RAISING OZARK

Richard J. Stephens Jr., MA

Ozark Publishing

Contents

Chapter 1

Acknowledgment

L ife, absent my children would be a place void of purpose. From the moment I caught a glimpse of Natalie's face, turned, and saw Lilli reaching out for comfort, and watched Riyann belly laugh at one of momma's jokes, I knew my destiny. Life is a journey, they say, and Natalie Banks (Stephens), Lilli Stephens and Riyann Stephens have given this journey value and design. Thank you for the hugs and smiles, tears, and encouragement along the way ladies. I am eternally proud to be called your dad.

Chapter 2

Introduction

Putting pen to paper and memorializing events and discoveries through writing was always a notion far removed from my mind. In fact, my father disclosed to me several years prior to his death that he recalled an occasion where he was contacted by one of my primary school teachers, voicing their concern over my perceived inability to communicate through written form. Their fear was I would be unable to effectively communicate in our modern society unless drastic measures were taken. In the humble manner, only my father could consistently portray, he simply assured her that I would succeed just fine as soon as I found my voice. Never again was a word spoken about the issue until more than thirty years later.

Seemingly, my father knew that hidden deep inside me, the true person would be reveled one day. Until approximately fifteen years ago, one would seldom find my written words and even less common hear me speak of my beliefs and feelings relating to current events. I somberly went about my life, interacting as anyone would, reclusive by nature but constantly striving to find and spotlight the good in everyone I came in contact with.

As I matured, I found that the outward, clean cut, professional good guy characteristics could co-exist with the fun, let it all hang out, goofy side, restrained deep inside. I credit my daughters fully for helping me understand the benefits to letting go and unleashing my true self upon the world.

Years later, I was approached by a regional newspaper editor who asked if I would consider writing a column for their newspaper. Their desire was that I share my experiences as they related to my children and being a parent. Upon agreeing I embarked upon a journey of not only discovery but likewise of enlightenment, while engaging my audience. I found that my life truly was enhanced through the mere existence of my children and within each experience, silly action, hug, and smile lessons could be learned which would benefit all mankind.

Each human experiences potentially life altering, or enhancing, events which many times go un-realized because of a wide array of reasons, if realized, can be a guide for fulfillment and success. This simple journey, "Raising Ozark" and my earlier "Tales from the Dad Side Articles" are merely an expression of one man's learning how to begin the process of recognizing and applying those events in our lives in hopes that true joy, understanding, and happiness will result.

Sit back, grab some refreshments, and embark upon this journey with me as we draw wisdom from one of the most challenging yet rewarding occupation there is... being a parent.

Chapter 3

A Gift with Meaning

G rowing up in the midwestern United States, I was taught to be a man's man, working hard, respecting everyone, and ultimately placing God first, family second, and work and everything else flowing from there. My father routinely taught me to get back up when I stumbled, rub some dirt on the scrapes and to rarely show emotion; for that could potentially reveal weakness. He imparted upon me that there were times when a man must drop the proverbial shield of emotionless adherence and cover ourselves with the cloak of emotion; those times were reserved for the times we were helping others or feeling great loss.

During the heat filled days of summer, while engaged in my final year as the elected Sheriff in Missouri, I recall my youngest daughter swiftly moving towards me. She had been playing with the latest gift she had received from a family member. You know, the gifts which are not so welcome, by us parents, due to the mass amount of work we have to put into it to "help". The gifts that our beloved family members bestow upon our kids as a sort of unspoken payback for some long before deed, deserving of the ultimate punishment. Those gifts which we accept with a smile but down deep inside we begin planning the ultimate revenge gift which can be given to their kids next Christmas.

As my girl got to where I was seated, she reached out and gave me a blue and pink, rope bracelet with the letters "DAD" affixed, with beads. "Let me see your hand" she said as she tied a series of knots on the string ensuring that the string was firmly attached to my wrist. She explained that I was the best and that her gift, the result of all her hard work, would remind me that she loved me.

As I gazed upon the brightly colored emblem of a seven-year-olds love and affection, I couldn't help but think about how my wrist was beginning to resemble a 80's hair band reject, adorned with brightly colored "bling". My "dad band" had been one in a series of body adornments she had provided for her dear ol dad, and my mind wondered to the fact that I would be returning to work, assuredly the subject of much ridicule from my co-workers.

At that moment I decided that what truly mattered was not conformity to some unwritten code or ensuring that I resembled everyone else but rather the love a child has for her father and his willingness to display the symbol of her love, regardless of the cost. In my child's mind she gave me the ultimate expression of her love and my failing to display it would bring much disgrace. Did my friends look upon me with a devious smile, planning their next good-hearted joke or action, absolutely. Did it matter in the scope of things, absolutely not.

Sometimes, bringing joy to others as they attempt to bring you blessings and brand you as their own is monumental. Showing them, you appreciate their actions even though you may get a bit of good hearted ribbing is worth it. My daughter still checks, daily, to see if I am wearing my gift. Now, a year later, you will still find it on my wrist, a token of not only a daughters love but of a man's willingness to accept even the things which can bring him unease for the betterment of the whole tribe.

Although petite in nature, this little band has withstood the test of time and remains intact. Just as the bond is between parent and child. I have become accustomed to it and would be sad if I didn't feel or see it. On my wrist.

Life Lessons

Be willing to step out of your comfort zone occasionally my friends. For when you do; you, as I have, will surely find calm in your moment of storm and happiness through letting down your walls of normality.

Chapter 4

Spread Kindness like Glitter

As my daughters and I were preparing to leave the house for a day of school and work I noticed that my nine-year-old; Lilli had dressed up a little more formal than normal. Adorned in a beautiful white and gold dress, she sported the product of her lengthy preparation including curls and a touch of makeup. It was unknown exactly why she chose her special dress that day, maybe it was simply to feel a little bit more special, or possibly a young boy had caught her eye and she was ready to impress. Regardless I complimented her, and of course carried out my fatherly duty by warning her of the dangers of contact with boys who surely had "cooties", and we went about our business.

Dropping the girls off at school went as planned, without a hitch and as my girls walked away from the car and disappeared behind the walls of their little school building my heart felt joy at the thought of what great young ladies, they each were becoming. Apprehensive at the thought that I would soon be tasked with the chore of running off any and all gentlemen suitors, I was happy. Once securely inside, I departed and went about my normal duties. Later, pushing myself up to my computer monitor, adjusting in the seat to ensure I had the perfect positioning for comfort; I observed what appeared to be a single, glimmering object on my hand.

As I looked closer, I noted that somehow, I had attracted a tiny piece of gold colored glitter. Considering it odd, I did my best to brush the glitter off my hand and carry on. As the day went on, I continued finding small pieces of glitter, seemingly reproducing with no sight of a source. Perplexed yet unconcerned I completed my daily tasks and carried on. It wasn't until several days later, seemingly a factory full of glitter discovered and frustration brewing that the source of the glitter explosion reveled itself.

Seated in my vehicle, some unknown force caused me to turn and investigate the back passenger seat. There lied the source of my sparkling nemesis. Peering upon the seat, shimmering in the sunlight, was a multitude of golden glitter. Then it hit me, Lilly's dress, which she chose to wear that fateful day was decorated with beautiful lines and flowers. The only problem was those same lines and flowers were nothing more than glitter affixed to the garment with glue. When she sat down to travel to school, she unknowingly transferred her sparkling demeanor, through the glitter, to my car seat. From there you can imagine, as any parent knows, glitter is long lasting and somehow never ending.

So here I sit, covered in glitter, watching as seemingly every inch of my vehicle has taken on new, disco like appearance; with no option but to smile. Months have passed, yet the glitter remains and now the beautiful dress has been passed on to her younger sister.

Life Lessons

Putting the glitter incident in perspective, I came across a statement the other day while carousing on social media. I read as a friend posted a meme which simply said, "spread kindness like glitter". I must admit, I instantly smiled at the thought. So often, we find frustration in the little things, the mishaps, the inconveniences. What an impact we would have in our communities if we simply were kind, an unrelenting kindness visible and seemingly unable to be removed. Realistic? Why not? We, my friends control our behavior and like glitter; have the means by which displaying kindness to others attaches itself, spreading to every surface.

Chapter 5

Swimming with the Fish

L ast year, midway through the summer tourist season, my wife and I were speaking with one of our guests. Being the owner of a small roadside Motel has emboldened us to meet new people, while learning a great deal about other cultures and the places to go see and those to stay away from while visiting other communities. This guest described that a neighboring community had "the best coconut cream pie" a person could eat. Now, being a large man and a connoisseur of sweets, I determined we needed to try this place out to ensure we weren't getting false information.

Midway through our adventure we came across a quaint, mid-sized lake, ripe with recreational possibilities. We later returned and watched as the girls played while swimming, enjoying the natural beauty of their lake-based adventure. While watching the girls enjoy their time away, Leona, my wife, and I began talking about how we enjoyed this solitude and how it would be perfect to have a boat to add to the enjoyment. As time passed, the desire grew and within a week, I was standing on the bow of our new, slightly used pontoon, trying to recall all of the nautical rules from my Navy days, seemingly a lifetime ago.

The family purchase brought with it excitement and to be honest a bit of angst and uncertainty. The concept of floating around, lighting up a BBQ and soaking in the sun, while the girls played nearby was easy enough. Ensuring everyone's safety and the proper operation of the vessel was a bit of a stressor considering it had been a easy twenty five years since I operated a boat on navigable waters. Regardless, we began living the experience, weekly, which brought joy and excitement to each of us.

Following several weeks of "lake time" our family discovered the true joy of simply centering on the adventure and fittingly named our vessel "L&R squared- Unplugged". The girls became more and more adventurous with their play on and off the boat and began venturing further from the safety of the rails as they swam. I recall a moment when it was difficult to maintain my composure, while simultaneously attempting to. Stay on the captain's chair as I laughed uncontrollably.

You see, our two daughters are similar in most ways; yet differ greatly in others. Our youngest, the adventurer, has made more emergency room visits and bore the scars of mishaps seemingly as symbolic badges of honor from her conquests. From the first instance we anchored the boat and gave them the go ahead, she jumped right in, caring not what lay beneath her, only concerned with the moment in time and her overcoming the unknown.

Lilli, on the other hand is our analytical, safety minded, safe child. Although she readily embarks upon adventures, it is only after she has researched fully, evaluated all possible outcomes, and has considered all possible ramifications of her choice, that she will dive in

.

On the day which found me falling out of my chair, wanting ever so badly to explain exactly what was going on. The girls asked if they could swim to the shoreline and collect shells. Being anchored approximately twenty five yards off shore, we gladly consented and the girls started they journey. Following a brief time and multiple shells discovered, their interest wained and they began their journey back to the boat. As the girls began their retreat, I could hear them talking. Lilli was for some reason talking to her sister about what possible living things could be swimming around them. One could hear the anxiety in her voice but she continued onward. Approximately half way between the shore line and the boat, I observed what appeared to be a large school of fish, disrupting the surface of the water nearby. In the normal dad way, I simply gained the attention of my wife and stated "wanna see something funny"?

The school of fish rapidly changed their direction and as Lilli swam, I noted that the two were on a collision course and in a matter of moments, their paths would intersect. Watching on, grins affixed, we listened as Lilli described to her sister that water safety was a must and if she felt a fish nibbling on her; she would not like it and for all practical purposes would be done exploring this lake based adventure. At that precise moment the school of little fish met Lilli, in the water. As she swam, never ceasing to talk, she felt the fish all around her as they swam by, she rapidly changed her tone to one of apprehension and concern and revealed "I don't know what that was and I really don't want to know" and continued on.

Arriving back at the boat, Lilli revealed that something weird happened in the water but overall she had fun. After revealing that she would remain on top of the water for a while we jokingly described what she experienced and how harmless the school was. She laughed and explained that she was not in fear, but ensured us she felt remaining topside was the most prudent action at this point.

Life Lessons

As I reminisce about that fun family time I am reminded about how many times in life we cross paths with the unknown. Our lives tend to be rattled with ups and downs and commonly intersect with things which bring us fear, anger, or simply emboldens our anxiety. As with Lilli, simply keeping paddling, never ceasing to remain focused on finish line, will bring us home safely. Since that time, Lilli has regained her willingness to dive in and experience all that the lake and life has to offer.

Paddle on my friends; regardless of what surrounds us.

Chapter 6

The Value of Joy

I have found over the years that there truly is nothing like experiencing the joy of a child, and their honest, unabridged emotions at the precise moment they are overwhelmed with happiness. Maybe the joy derives from the newest toy, trip to a special place, or obtaining the latest trend worthy hair doo. Regardless, the inner fluttering which results is classic and worth much more than any amount of money. I have been blessed to witness it on several occasions.

My first experience watching pure joy took me by surprise. My daughter, Natalie and I spent much of her youth doing whatever we could to find happiness, despite the fact that financially we were strapped. Although unable to provide some of the nicer things in life, I truly never really recognized the fact that we were not exactly poor by the worlds eyes but unable to do more than put food on the table at times. We struggled through each day but always found a way to find happiness in a pure form of father daughter love. Finding adventures to stimulate the mind such as photographic adventures, hiking through the Colorado mountains, and singing along with the latest top ten radio artist became our norm.

As a single parent, at the time, there were many things that although I wanted to provide to my child, some were simply unobtainable. This bothered me but as the majority of us know, we simply make the best of it and carry on, attempting to mask our inward, inadequate feelings of being the parent who couldn't give his child everything they want.

When Natalie was approximately eleven or twelve years old, she decided she wanted to take part in the latest fashion trend. She did her research, spoke to her mother, and decided that her long, straight brown hair needed an upgrade. Approaching me with her vision, she ensured me that the entire process of turning straight hair into curls through getting a perm would be painless and would in fact; drastically increase her standing within her peer circle. Wanting to bring happiness to my child I agreed but found it necessary to do some research on my own. Following discovering that the process had no negative ramifications for a child her age I agreed.

Following a short time of saving the funds necessary, she and I embarked upon this latest adventure. After making the forty- mile journey to our salon of choice I entered the doorway of the one area most men avoid... the dreaded hair salon. Luckily, it was early in the day so the peering eyes from the ladies, adorned in tin foil covered locks, gowns, and other things a man really shouldn't experience were minimal. As I found my seat my mind rapidly flowed to concern over the pungent smell emitting from what I assumed was one lady's hair, seemingly overtaking the entire structure. Recognizing my eminent state of shock and confusion, the beautician assured me everything was alright. Although I wasn't buying it fully, I reluctantly voiced my understanding, inwardly praying I survived this adventure, and reclined in what could only be described as the "scared man observer" chair, never escaping the laughing yet angry eyes of the tin foil adorned lady.

With air seeming in short supply, watering eyes from the chemicals, and concern for my personal safety because of the one lady who kept wanting me to sit in this huge pink chair and allow her access to my feet, to do whatever happens to one's feet in one of those place's, the words came I had been waiting for. We were done. Natalie received her new perm, and I was finally able to escape.

Quickly we paid for this latest adventure and rapidly exited the door. I will add, I'm relatively certain that as we exited, I saw the tin foil lady shake her head in agreement with her head slightly tilted upward in a evident manner to say, that's right you better run. Making it safely to our vehicle I remember looking over at Natalie asking her if she liked the final result. As I turned, I observed that she was shaking, uncontrollably, with the largest smile affixed to her face I had seen to date. She simply couldn't contain her joy and it burst out in her uncontrollable laughter. Instantaneously, my heart leapt as she stated, "I love it" and I realized that the struggle from the past hour and a half or so was worth it and bringing this type of joy to my child was from there on out my only goal in life.

Life Lessons

Thinking back, I learned that precious memories can be made regardless of your situation. many times, we affix joy and happiness to monetary things when in all reality it is the things we obtain, the things we do, which cost the least that many times reap the greatest rewards. I've found that the value obtained from taking part in the simpler things are priceless. Struggling is a part of life as is finding a way around the struggles. For it is when we place less emphasis on materials and more on the person or adventure that we truly are in a position to provide that much sought after gift, and receiving it means so much more.

Chapter 7

Unleash Your Individuality

My wife Leona and I were resting at the living quarters at the Motel a couple years ago while the girls were out of sight and to be truthful out of mind. It is a rarity in our home to have moments of silence due to Lilly's excessive storytelling and Riyann's adventuring spirit. Being coined with the nickname of "Chatterbox", Lilli finds great joy in verbally bombarding everyone she sees, upon every opportunity she come across, with the latest intelligence she has gathered from a wide variety of sources. On this day, Lilli was seemingly running low on the proverbial fuel for her information gathering so she was silently seated at the kitchen table, studying a book, ever diligently preparing for her next round of dispensing information to her family, ensuring they understood the ins and outs of whatever she was reading about.

Riy on the other hand was missing in action, which that in itself should have struck fear in the hearts of any care giver. To many emergency room visits, broken bones and utter destruction has resulted from her silence and exploration. I remember hearing a old truth, years ago which described that if you don't hear your children playing you must be prepared because they are definitely up to no good and world domination is the only thing on their minds. On this day we truly didn't care if the world was ran by a six year old genius or not. We were simply basking in the silence.

Our home is one of both; utter, hold onto your seat craziness, and yet, at times, pure solace from the most perfect correlation of a mechanism moving in perfect unison. Working together we all attempt to better each other while throwing in an adequate amount of humor through practical jokes, tickle sessions, and good hearted making fun of each other, while vehemently fighting to the end for one another if the need arose.

Reclining slightly, I heard movement from upstairs and looked toward my lovely wife with a kind of apprehensive gaze, attempting to prepare her for what we would soon discover; our youngest had been engaged in. Being smarter than I, she simply ignored me, in an apparent attempt to avoid eye contact. Little did I know that this simple act would allow her to avoid all parental accountability and help her put off the eventual truth that she would have to deal with the result forthcoming. With my attempts spoiled, to ensure she had adequate time to prepare for what we would surely be faced with in mere moments, the child made her way downstairs.

Bracing myself, yet intrigued at the possibilities, I placed a jovial smile on my face, ensuring that my child knew I was ready for anything and excited about discovering what she had created. To my dismay, ok, in all honesty, to my ever-growing elation, she rapidly passed my location and promptly walked up to her mother. Now I will say I performed the proverbial "Ca Ching" in my mind as I watched the payback for mommas ignoring my attempts to warn her.

As I watched Leona and Riyann's interaction out of the corner of my eye, I saw Leona look at me with a kind of bewildered look in her eye. With an emboldened curiosity I looked up as Leona asked, "Do you see what your child has done"? As I looked, I could see Riyann with a big, proud smile affixed to her face, holding a Barbie doll. I then watched as Leona lifted a second doll, pointing it in my direction. Attempting to shield my lack of observation I simply replied that her baby doll was very pretty.

Leona quickly asked, no, do you see what Riyann has done? It then hit me. The genius of this six-year-old child had surfaced. We discovered that the silence from the upstairs was not Riyann devising a scorched earth plan of domination, but rather her spending an hour designing a clothing line for her barbies out of balloons. Looking on with disbelief, Leona and I could do little but praise the ingenuity of the child. She had taken a concept she had dreamt of in her mind, found a medium by which to create and put her thoughts into action. After regaining our senses and lifting our jaws from the floor we asked Riyann where she saw this and how she learned to create these clothing lines from balloons. She simply said she "thought it up".

Life Lessons

So often we anticipate the worst possible result when we experience certain situations and people throughout our life. Maybe it is the person who has created angst in our mind, caused us stress, or simply doesn't see things the same as us. Maybe its confronting a situation we have failed at previously or simply feared engaging in. When we restrain our options completely, we fail to see the beauty which can result given a vision and a little hard work. Never restrain your dreams and natural abilities. Unleash your individuality for the world to see. For it is when we unleash them and put them on display that our progress is on full display and our actions can benefit another possibly unleashing their inner individuality.

Chapter 8

Choose Your Moments

I believe we can all agree that life, many times, is full of distractions, disasters, and mishaps, many designed to thrust us to our knees. Given our response, those moments can either have long lasting negative results or become the proving ground by which we see them as the building blocks empowering our eventual success. A Moment just like those became prevalent in my mind as I came across a photograph I had taken.

I was scrolling through the pictures on my telephone the other day when I came across a short video, I had made several years prior. The video was of my daughter Lilli, when she was merely one and a half years old. Although I will not get into great detail about the background of the videos content, I will provide our readers with a short synopsis to give you a glimpse into this powerful image.

You see, at the time the video was made, Lilli's life had been uprooted beyond belief and everything, other than her younger sister, she knew as stability, safety, and life had come crashing down as she was uprooted and placed in a situation foreign to her due to a tragedy. While standing in my wife and I's home, Lilli and hung out while my wife was tending to her little shop in town.

As I finished cleaning the dishes, I turned and couldn't help but pull out my phone, a action my children have come to distain. I began videoing her. Dressed in a cute blue nightgown, Lilli was tagging along exhibiting remarkable behavior. As I directed Lilli to smile, she simply reached upward with her hand, unwilling to voice a word, seemingly asking for nothing other than a little help into my arms. Dropping my camera immediately, I obliged the child, and all was well with the world, for both of us, as we danced around the kitchen.

Watching the video now, thinking about everything that had transpired over the span of a week when the video was made, seems to take on two very similar yet different meanings. First, one can see the outreaches hands of one in need. Lilli simply needed comfort and reassurance. Secondly, one can see, from the video, Lilly's Olympic moment of overcoming.

When I describe an Olympic moment, I do not refer to the Olympic sporting events most of us have come to love and honor but that of the sister ship to the Titanic, the RMS Olympic and a correlation I had heard about prior. The ocean liner Olympic had a long career spanning between 1911 and 1935. Prior to the Titanic she was the largest passenger liner with many of the world's greatest amenities for her time. Not unlike the Titanic, she was faced with multiple hardships, including collisions, war, attacks, and explosions. The disasters and changes experienced by the Olympia caused her to correct her course and overcome, numerous times, in order to succeed in a manner, the Titanic was unable to.

Life Lessons

We all seem to face those moments which require us to step back and evaluate which direction we are destined to proceed. Will we have a Titanic moment which destroys us and sends us sinking into oblivion. Or will we overcome the obstacles within our path and turn them into successes. Will we reach out our hand, longing for the grasp of support, love and stability. Likewise, will we recognize when others reach out their hands. Will we take hold of our brothers and sisters in this life and lift another up from what could be their Titanic moment?

May we ever be cognizant of the importance of being there for our fellow citizens, showing a willingness to recognize that extended hand of need, and subsequently extending your own to grab hold and lift others up. As we face the darkens and have to determine if they will become Titanic or Olympic moments, my only hope is that I can face them as Lilli has, not seeing them as absolute failures, with no hope of succeeding, but as Olympic possibilities.

Chapter 9

Expect the Unexpected

As summer bears down upon us, I was reminded yesterday that the holiday season is right around the corner. Advertisements telling us or rather warning us that Christmas was merely one-hundred-thirty-five days away seemingly brought with them a wide array of emotion. My mind almost instantaneously wondered to a series of events which took place in 2019.

As with any year, the holiday season brings with it great memories and thoughts of the future. Memories from the year prior remain etched in our mind as we look forward to the New Year. I, like many, gaze with apprehensive eyes. For with each new day, we expect the same while hoping for brighter horizons. We seemingly cannot avoid apprehension as others voice their intentions of creating a better path, making more viable choices, or even turning the page on a story seemingly written as a endless rerun.

Regardless of our intentions, be it our attempt to create a more productive self, or to view others in a more empathetic light we are seemingly forced to confront our own pessimistic thoughts as the days pass us by. We must guard ourselves from the reoccurring pattern of contentment which can many times overtake our desires for success and render us expecting little more than routine conformity to the skeletons of our past. As quoted by Heraclitus, a Greek philosopher, "If you do not expect the unexpected you will not find it, for it is not to be reached by search or trial".

Although, I many times set out with the purest intentions with the dawn of each new day, I, many times, falter and fail to see the good, or expect more than the norm. I was forced to confront my own pessimism awhile back, at the hands of my six-year-old daughter, at the time. My youngest is well known to be the highly motivated comedian who gives minimal thought to conforming to the everyday rules and procedures known as societal norms. Rather, she normalizes experiences and her adventurous exploration, while thinking outside the box. It is not uncommon for her to develop a solution out of the air like the 80's television hit, MacGyver, all the while bearing a smile large enough to melt any questioning heart.

My child, in 2019, decided she wanted a "bunny" rabbit and commenced stopping at every wishing well, and Santa Clause within the lower Missouri region over that year voicing her request. I'm certain she even put more pressure on by voicing her request during her nightly prayers of thanks. Now understand, her parents were not overly keen on the idea of an additional, living creature in the house, having even gone so far as requesting the short life span model through the local pet store. To our dismay, and through a barrage of store worker laughter, we came to discover those models were nonexistent.

The decision, following some soul searching, was made to answer the child's request, and allow Santa to deliver the new family member on Charismas Eve in 2019. My wife and I fully expected the little white bundle of joy to carry with it a day or two's excitement then become like many of the other items, merely another chore for daddy or older sister to daily engage in until its eventual expiration.

Here I sit, years later, bewildered at the resilience of not only little "Fluffy" the rabbit, but with my child. Where I was certain she would falter and loose interest, she and her sister have remained committed. Where I expected the battle of responsibility, they have maintained and exceeded. Where I hoped, but maintained little faith, my children have educated me. My child has proven herself and although short in duration, has stepped up to the plate and become a responsible caregiver.

Now, what remains? What is big ol dad left with other than a renewed vision of expecting not only what is expected but additionally what is unexpected. Yes, you guessed it, her sister voicing her intent on pressuring Santa for a Hedge Hog... where on earth does one find a hedgehog?

Life Lessons

Life, it seems, is riddled with the unexpected. If we merely open our eyes to the ultimate possibilities and the basic resilience of the human desire, we may just watch the unexpected unfold before our eyes.

Chapter 10

Awakening the Bear

I f we are honest with ourselves, anyone who has had the pleasure of having a child in their home has been confronted with situations where it took everything you had to hold back the laughter for the betterment of the situation. I experienced one such moment a couple years ago, which still causes me to break out in laughter at the mere thought of the situation.

It was not abnormal in our household on that fateful day. The day came with fun, laughter, and a rather large amount of our children avoiding their chores at all costs. Any parent knows the difficulties which are the result of trying to get your kids to clean up anything let alone their bedrooms. On this date, momma made it plain that the girls needed to get their bedroom cleaned up and our youngest needed to stop procrastinating and get her hair brushed. Plainly it was stated that failure to comply would result in the loss of their beloved iPads or some similar devastating punishment which would surely bring on the end of the world in the child's mind.

Mid way through my wife giving the girls some direction, Momma directed our youngest child to get upstairs and get her hair brushed. This simple request, although not unreasonable, didn't sit well with the child and she, in a seemingly opening of the floodgates, began breathing heavily, and although she turned towards her bedroom, she remained standing, unmovable, in a kind of momentary thought of just how far she was willing to take this battle.

You know the kind of look which although no sane father would ever admit publicly, was a look which brought about fear. The look when seeing it from a woman, the man would be best served by simply stepping back, regrouping, and finding a way to appease the beast which was brewing and preparing to go forth throughout the land destroying all who were in its path. Yeah, that look of a warrior preparing for battle with the ultimate mission of total devastation... that was the look on my seven-year-old princesses face.

As the cold sweats continued, I recognized that my fatherly duties including taking a hard stance and being as supportive as possible, to my wife, to ensure my continued survival and to ensure the warrior face didn't transfer from my child to my beloved wife. As I rose my child had seemingly made the decision to begin walking upstairs in an apparent form of compliance with her mother's wishes. As I silently walked behind my child, she was unaware of my presence.

As I entered the doorway to the stair well my child was approximately halfway up the stair case. I silently watched as she made her way up the stairs, stomping heavily to ensure her mother was well aware of her displeasure. It was at that moment that I lost all ability to continue onward. As I entered the stairwell I could hear my child, conversing with herself. Simply said she reiterated to herself, angrily, that she was not doing it and she didn't care what "mom said". Hearing those words stopped me in my path. Looking back, I am unsure if the words stopped me because truly, it was funny to hear the child find her voice through frustration as it burst forth because in her mind brushing her hair wasn't important, or if it was the fact that the child hasn't learned the art of avoiding angering the momma bear.

In the end, Riy's hair got brushed, the room got cleaned, and Leona and I had a good laugh about our child's words and actions. To this day, I think about the incident and think about how many valuable lessons I am afforded because of this thing called parenting.

Life Lessons

Throughout this journey called life we are confronted with decisions regarding tasks we are asked to complete and requested others make of us. Some are valid, some in our minds are ludicrous. Regardless, our decision to or not to comply bears with it a result. Sometimes it's simply inconvenience and sometimes its awakening the bear. Avoid awakening the bear while remaining true to yourself.

Chapter 11

Fight Through the Fear

Growing up along the front range of Colorado I was never really all that jazzed about this time of year, when school would commence again for the new year. I would always look forward to the first day with excitement because of the unknown and the change in settings, but those feelings were normally short lived once the daily routine set in and the work began.

This week I learned a valuable lesson from the girls. The girls, although separated by a little over a year, in age, are similar in many ways and vastly different in many more. Lilli is an exponentially analytical thinker who loves school and the learning which is at her fingertips. Riyann, not so much so. Riy thrives off her artistic fervor and her ability to engineer exciting new concepts with minimal effort. Over the years we have learned that Riyann for the most part despises school and has become somewhat a recluse when attending.

A couple of weeks ago Leona and I were shocked when Riy was describing that she was ready for school to start this year. Apparently, our shock was visible upon our faces hence, Riyann quickly backtracked and explained that she was not really that excited about school. As the days passed, we continued to attempt to encourage the girls through describing what an awesome year this will be and the possibilities they would be experiencing with new grades and new teachers.

The normal routine within our family is like prepping for a battle of sorts. Repeated warnings, threats, and frustration filled the air as we attempt to get the little one up and ready for a day of schooling, which she despised, and the quiet hugs and encouragement routinely given upon her returning home with tears in her eyes from her inability to fit the student mold effectively. Although honestly, numerous attempts to influence her thoughts on school and providing her encouragement, we felt the strain of how best to set our child up for success given her outlook.

Earlier this week, while viewing a social media post, I observed a notice that the school was having a back-to-school fair. Attempting to excite the girls, I jovially passed on the information and to my surprise both girls were moderately excited about their attendance. We attended the schools back to school festivities where the girls would have the opportunity to see their new classrooms and meet their teachers. Although Riyann tagged along, the original excitement over the event faded and she displayed no outward signs of elation or happiness. As we approached the building Riyann explained that she was nervous. Following some encouragement, we passed through the doorway and things quickly changed.

Seeing one of Riyann's "friend teachers" she quickly ran to her. I had to laugh inwardly because as Riyann approached the teacher, she started running then instantaneously in an apparent form of restraint from remembering that it was not acceptable to run in school, began speed walking like an Olympic gold medalist, towards the teacher giving her a huge hug upon her arrival. The teacher reciprocated Riyann excitement a, returning her hug with selfless vigor, loving on the child, and welcoming her to a bright new year.

This scene played its way out repeatedly all the way down the hallway, as we passed each classroom doorway. A smile became fixed to my child's face as she explored her new classroom and spoke to her new teacher. Lilli, feeling a bit apprehensive herself because of her move into a different building due to her age, likewise quickly calmed as excitement overtook her while exploring her new environment. Upon returning home the girls, both, were full of excitement and energy as they showed their grandmother the newest items they had received and told her all about the cool new things they saw this night. As my wife described "It is all right with their world now". The same can be said about mom and dad as well.

Life Lessons

As I considered this monumental day for the girls I am reminded about how often we draw conclusions about people and situations and those same conclusions restrain our future actions somewhat. In many cases our feelings or insight into others is the result of our experiences and or our misconceptions. When we show a willingness to step out of the shelter of our mind and simply run /walk towards new adventures, with purpose, it is then that we restrain the fear within us and experience a more inclusive life.

Chapter 12

Find Your Calling

Growing up in the mid-west brought with it many opportunities for fantasizing about future accomplishments and the roles I may someday fill. Whether it was dreaming of the mountain men of old, sports hero's or professionals in the spotlight a young person could find inspiration and begin setting the tone for where their aspirations would eventually lead them. I never dreamed that one day my daughter would describe that she was worried about my retiring and my no longer being "famous". I never truly understood that while I tried to bring my children the best life possible, in their eyes, I was a superhero.

As the years have passed this old boy by, accomplishments have been realized and positions of importance held, as with many who look back on their life and think about where they have been. Looking back, I have come to realize that my true calling in life was far from what I had dreamed of as a young man. Without even striving in that direction, I was thrust into leadership roles, routinely, early in my adult life which would eventually become foundational.

Over the years, I have lead people, municipalities, counties, and organizations. I've owned businesses and been broke. I have fed the homeless, spoke to large conference groups and small teams. I held the dying while at times prepared to take a life while preserving many others. I calmly stroked the face of the dying while calming them as they walked toward the beautiful lights of heaven. I've fought for my life and the lives of my brothers while restraining the fear of war.

I've tasted meals more expensive than my rent and opened meals not fit to consume. I've walked the halls of power and those of desolation. I've lived and let live, while always striving to better myself and those around me.

As I consider this journey called life, I've came to realize that the calling I was created for was not one of status, fortune, or notoriety but one of true service to those precious, vulnerable ones around us. My calling is simply to be a dad.

This calling has led me down the path of joy and tears, happiness and terror. It has allowed me to fully experience a love so deep, exploration would be impossible if it were put into literal terms. It has allowed me to rise to a height grander than the peaks of the Rocky Mountains and feel lower than the deepest depths of the ocean because of my failures. It has come through both surprise and through choice.

I have become a superhero in my children's eyes, sitting through countless hours of games, concerts, and recitals, forcing a smile simply to bring joy to my children. I've played games when I didn't feel like it, and laughed at jokes that weren't funny simply to bring joy to a child. I watch as my daughters have designed clothing out of balloons and solved problems which make me ponder why. I've held the tired and mended the broken, only to start it all over again tomorrow, hoping so diligently that their eyes would awaken to a brighter day.

Some ask why I would give up the power and status. Some cannot understand why I wouldn't desire that. To sit next to those in power and look upon the starry-eyed onlookers as they contemplate their own aspirations. To me, I've loved my life, and enjoyed the journey. To the world I may not be much now but through the eyes of my daughters I still wear a cape and I am everything and that is right where I want to be.

Life Lessons

Regardless of which path this life has led us down or the things we strive to accomplish, if a child is part of that equation, we must understand the lenses by which they are viewing you through. Meet your goals, obtain the heights you have set but forget not that you, and you alone are many times a child's sole example of value. Take the time to engage them, get on the floor. And play. Be silly yet serious. I have no doubt that when you do, you will see eyes filled with wonder, admiration, and longing pearling back at you. At that moment, it is then that you will truly be the most important person in this world.

Chapter 13

Bringing you Down

Throughout history the struggle between the young and old has been a visual reminder of generational differences. Although fostering phenomenal relationships with my children, we have not been absent the occasional disagreement and friction. I recall several years ago my eldest daughter decided she desired to become the owner of a cuddly little kitten. Although not my dream pet, I relented, and we welcomed the furry little feline into the fold.

As we carried about our normal routine of work and school the kitten grew alongside my child and its older sibling cat; my daughter had adopted many years before. "Kitty" the older cat quickly grew weary of the newest family member and would routinely seclude herself to a perch from which she could watch with a condescending look while not having to be a party to the latest adventures the littlest family member was engaging in.

As the time passed by, we noticed something quite odd about Natalie's little bundle of furry joy. Regardless of the situation, the cat would have an evil smirk on its little face and glare as if it was strategizing on how this little four-pound feline was going to end your existence. I'm convinced the pet had serious emotional issues but regardless my child still loved the little beast although she was growing weary of its antics.

When the little beast was approximately four months old, I believe I came to understand the core of the problem. I became convinced that some evil demon had infiltrated the kitty who had the outward appearance of radiant sunshine and warmth but inwardly was consumed with meanness and bad intentions. You laugh now but truly, should a man have to watch his back in his own home, because of a fear of what evil lurks beyond the hallway in the form of your beloved daughters skinny, juvenile cat?

My beliefs became incontestable when one day while preparing for work, I was standing in front of the bathroom mirror. Following completing my morning ritual, I took a moment to say a quick prayer asking for the safety of my family and my willingness to live a servant type life towards others. Out of nowhere, the furry Satan spawn turned the corner and sprung towards me grasping my leg. Containing my leg in a fierce grasp by utilizing both of his front arms, mouth and whatever else the beast could find. It's actions were apparently designed to ensure any attempted escape, on my part, was futile.

Following a short battle, I escaped and was left with a confused mind and somewhat speechless demeanor over what had just occurred. Although I could see the cats end in sight I battled forward due to my child's love for this truly evil being. Over the next couple months, the cat calmed somewhat with the exception of when it caught you praying. If it saw, you pray it leapt into action and the apparent evil inside would spring forth into a sort of scorched earth form of action.

In the end, the cat found a new home, Natalie was happy, and dads legs healed although the emotional toll brought on by the beast may remain a lifetime. I've heard he became a farm cat which would suit him well and I'm sure bring him countless hours of joy as he hunted the countryside. My only hope is that whichever farm he resides upon, that no poor soul decides to take a moment to sit along the tree line to have a quick devotional and prayer. For if they do I have no doubt they will be in for a surprise at the hands of the evil demon cat.

Life Lessons

As I ponder on my experiences with Natalie's little bundle of joy, I am reminded about how many times the external factors in our life seemingly try their best to bring us down and stop us from walking the line we have chosen. When we feel things, relationships, and situations are perfect and our lives are where they need to be, just like the cat, it at times, instantaneously transforms into a beast bent on destroying your peace and prosperity. We must maintain focus and carry on understanding that we, and we alone are in control of our destiny. As the external, and at times internal factors surface, fight them off, tend your scratches, continue along your path as you find happiness in the knowledge that you and you alone will prevail to greatness.

Chapter 14

The Fine Art of Being a Table

L ife, at times can appear overwhelming. As we travel this path of seemingly never-ending hardship, disaster, and proverbial downs it's difficult to keep sight of the
positive things surrounding us. Recently my community suffered the loss of one of our
major businesses. This on the feet of recent historic disasters left many with the inner
feeling of how much more can one be asked to bare.

While strolling through photographs, reminiscing about all the good times my family
have enjoyed at the business, I came across a photo that not only brought a smile to my
face but likewise a calmness to my heart. The photo was simply a shot my wife had taken
of my youngest daughter and I. Captured within the content of the photo was a father
resting on his child while she was deeply engaged in viewing the latest video she so enjoyed.

As I viewed the photograph I was reminded about the importance of meeting others
at their time and place of not only need but of enjoyment. Many times, we become
self-centered and merely wish to engage in things that we wish to do and we forget about
the importance of reciprocating joy and embarking upon true interaction outside our
preferred realm.

While engaged in my graduate level studies, I recall learning about the importance of
getting on your children's level and taking the time to play their games. This willingness
shows the child that they, and the things they choose to do, has importance to the

parent and hence establishes validity. I believe the concept goes much deeper than merely showing importance.

As a young youth minister in Aurora Colorado, I remember speaking to young people about our program and all the adults who chose to help with events, outings, and meetings. I recall one specific group of young people who described that certain leaders cared about them and some did not. Interested in understanding, I inquired as to why they felt certain leaders didn't care for them. That was when one young lady simply said... "because you love us".

The fact that I cared for the children was not a revelation more was it not readily viewable but what set me back was the fact that the kid's felt the other leaders did not care. Feeling that the children were incorrect at their assertion I asked them to tell me why they felt that way and one of the young ladies simply said, "because you spend time with us... your time shows your love".

Life Lessons

Life itself is a series of choices. How we decide to engage with others, although on the surface bears very little significance, really has utmost importance. As with a father resting on the lap of his child while she is engaged shows a willingness to become secondary to her desire for connection. The mother playing on the floor with her son as they hold action figures and trucks, a skill she may not have perfected and truly doesn't enjoy, holds major significance to her offspring.

Likewise, taking the time to engage those around you in their favorite moment and ventures can enhance our ability to create community and ultimately show others that their choices are important and valid. For it is when we are quick to engage, slow to disrupt, and willing to explore that true love and understanding can result. Don't be afraid to hit the floor, play some games, and meet others at their place of joy. In doing so we will find true healing and lasting understanding that although life can be cruel at times, the future is bright and open for adventure.

Trust me, being a table, even for a moment in time, is the most awesome thing.

Chapter 15

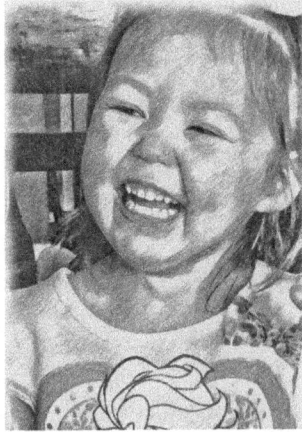

Absorbing the Wisdom

Fatherhood, although the most awesome journey one can embark upon, is riddled with moments when all you can do is stand in amazement as you do your best to hold back the unavoidable laughter which has been brewing and quickly reaching a point of overflowing because of the actions of your offspring. Allowing your child to save face while you attempt to lift them up through their disasters and find the proverbial light at the tunnel is challenging when all you want to do is point and laugh... and maybe throw in a fatherly "I told you so". This past week I experienced one such moment.

Recently, Lilli, my nine-year-old has been constantly doing her best to convince her mother that she needed to transition into the next phase of life and shave her legs. Although, hesitant at first, we decided that the constant pleas and nine-year-old reasoning were becoming reasonable. Against all my fatherly instincts, and my wife's reluctance, we for the lack of a better word "caved". Her mother began the process of demonstrating the fine art of shaving one's lower legs, while setting strict boundaries and ensuring all safety protocols were adhered to. Doing well, Lilli listened intently and became a proficient user of double -bladed razor, not believing that she would one day regret her decision to begin the process so early, as her mother assured her would happen.

The joy of having multiple children and the excitement of knowing that momma and daughter were engaged in this special bonding adventure quickly hit me and left this father frazzled at the thought of what was soon to come considering his little one was now beginning the process of shaving her legs. This in combination with my ever-resilient dad ears hearing about dating boys and "love stories" simply reiterated the fact that I must now prepare for the pending boy apocalypse in and around my home, which was surly soon to come.

Lest I forget, this process included our sneaky child acting as if she had no desire to take part in the process her sister, one and a half years elder, was embarking upon. Although this discussion took place merely a few months prior, Riyann has never voiced a desire to follow the same path of her sister and the razor. Although strange, I felt relieved that at least one of my babies would remain a child for as long as she could hold out.

This past week brought that concept, firmly held in my mind, to a screeching halt. As I woke up the girls and hurriedly plead with them to get ready for school, I noticed that Riyann was attempting to brush her hair with a hoody on and head covered. As I directed her to remove her hood she reluctantly did so. I gave it no more thought and we quickly went about our preparations. Dropping them off at school, we said our daily I love you's and off they went to conquer the educational world.

Upon returning that afternoon I noticed Lilli was outwardly upset but ensured me she was fine when I inquired as to what was wrong. We then returned to the motel where I began working on some maintenance issues, when my dynamic duo came to the room and described that they needed to speak to me in private. With great big elephant tears in her eyes, Riyann remained silent as Lilli described that they needed to speak to me, but I couldn't tell anyone what they were about to reveal. Following some prompting, Riy began describing that she "just wanted to be like" her sister. She then explained that the night prior, while showering she decided that she was going to shave her legs, like her big sister, knowing that her mom told her not to, and she "accidently" shaved off half of her eyebrows. Attempting to reconcile how her eyebrow was removed while shaving her lower legs proved pointless, hence, I simply listened intently while biting my cheek as to not outwardly bust out into laughter over the child's plight.

Between elephant tears she assured me that her mother was going to kill her, and she didn't know what to do because it truly was an accident. Holding back my laughter, I inspected the dreaded "accident" and explained that she would be alright and although definitely missing, she had only shaved half the brow and a bit of make-up would easily cover her self-imposed flaw. She gleefully agreed but quickly returned to the fact that her mother would definitely end her eight-year-old life over this incident and that she should have listened. I agreed that following her mother's direction was important and that although she made a mistake, her mother still loved her, and I was pretty certain her life would not end.

As Lilli and RIy hurried off to mend the brow with makeup I was finally able to release my caged-up emotion. As I rose from my laughter, momma entered the parking lot and seeing my smile asked me what was going on. Following my pleas of secrecy and of course her fun hearted agreeance, I relayed the story of our child's plight. As any good mother would do, she simply said she was going to laugh, and give her a hard time then tell her she should have listened. Riy survived. We joked and all had a few laughs at Riy's expense.

Life Lessons

As I look back, I am reminded about just how many times throughout life we disregard the directions and warnings of others as we attempt to pave our own path in life. We routinely disregard the fact that many times the path before us has already be flattened and if we merely listen and follow the wisdom of others our journey will be smoother. As an old friend once said to me "there's no sense in reinventing the wheel, use the wisdom which came before us and prosper from their work when necessary".

Chapter 16

Answers from Unexpected Places

Q uite often, I have noticed that our lives of being mothers and fathers are accompanied by moments of pure, unabridged, awe over things we see our children do. I for one have routinely been touched by the actions or words of my children. It seems that even though our kids consistently impress us there is always that proverbial "holy cow" moment, which reveals itself at the perfect time. One such time for me came last year as my family and I were on our annual "schools out for summer" outing.

For those of you who follow our writings about the girls will recognize that last year's outing included my families attempt to "unplug" ourselves from electronic devices and teach the girls about the important things in life. The adventure included our renting a rustic cabin along the shores of the Table Rock Lake. With very few modern amenities we were forced, or graced, depending on your outlook, to journey outside the norm, spending time conversing, playing board games, and wandering the forest simply finding solace in each other and nature.

One action my wife and the girls decided to take part in, during our adventure, was the fine art of assembling a puzzle. Little did I know, the trio had picked out the perfect, thousand-piece, puzzle during their initial shopping outings for supplies. I've been told that finding the perfect puzzle, with the perfect image was relatively simple with each girl agreeing. When asked about my excitement, which, according to the girls, was surely brewing about the inevitable fact that I would be helping assemble the puzzle, I had to think fast and develop a line of reasoning which would rid me of the eventual responsibility of taking part in the process. Not that I didn't think it would be a good idea, puzzles are simply not something I looked forward to.

As the evening fell upon us, my eldest child decided that it was the opportune moment to begin the assembly. Bearing a big smile on my face, and agreeing head shake, my mind rapidly began trying to come up with any acceptable excuse to not take part. To my dismay, the child was on her game and rapidly assembled the family leaving me with no choice but to partake in the dreaded monotony of bringing this image to life. Luckily, merely moments after we began, the trio recognized that good Ol dad was not adding, in a positive manner, to the process so when I gracefully stepped out for a bit they really didn't complain, nor did they invite me to re-engage.

Upon my return to the room, I watched as my wife and children had a blast finding the perfect piece and putting them all together. After a short time, my youngest lost interest and began planning her exit while the final two continued the struggle. As they continued, I routinely joked with my wife about the fact that like many things, there was probably one piece missing which they would not discover until they are almost done. Flashing that well known, close your mouth, look, I decided that it was in my best interest to watch in silence and simply enjoy the moment. The process of assembling the puzzle took two days. On the second day my wife revealed that I was in a moderate amount of trouble for "putting negativity" in the air because she had a nightmare the night prior about not finding one piece of the puzzle. Laughing, we simply kept the process going as I began encouraging the girls to continue. As I prepared the barbeque for our evening meal my wife came and revealed that I wouldn't believe what happened. As I inquired, she revealed that they had completed the entire puzzle. She asked if I wanted to know the best part to wit, I stated I would. It was then that she disclosed that the entire puzzle was done with the exception to the one piece which was missing.

Understanding that my next choice of words could be extremely important and more than likely life extending or shortening, I simply looked and said you must be kidding. Like a good husband, I immediately went to work checking everywhere, under things, and in-between items to locate the final piece of the puzzle. With no success I made the decision to quietly return to the barbeque and hope I survived the evening since it was me who "put that out there in the universe".

By the third day we could laugh, but truly were confused. With no one daring to move the treasured artwork, it sat as a visual reminder of hard work alongside frustration coupled with a tell- tell monument to a husband simply keeping his mouth shut. It was then that my wife turned to our youngest child and asked her if she had any idea where the missing piece of the puzzle could be. The child, excitedly rose to her feet and jumped into action in an apparent depiction of an athlete finally getting the call to help her team win. Without hesitation she quickly placed her hand to her mouth, in thought, and after a short time, moved towards the couch where she retrieved one small puzzle piece, a perfec t fit, finalizing all the hard work the family had done.

As we all simultaneously exhaled, my wife and I stood in amazement. My wife joked with the child, asking her if she hid the piece. The child assured her she had not but remembered, after being asked about the missing piece, that she saw a puzzle piece there the night before.

Life Lessons

Thinking back, I am reminded about how often we continue our journey of life, fo- cused on the missing piece rather than process by which it is assembled. In some cases, we spend hours taking the time to make all the pieces fit, all while simply hoping everything is available to us to complete the task. When we come across difficulty, or a missing piece our frustrations overwhelm us, rendering us somewhat useless in completing our task or feeling defeated. As with the puzzle piece, it is when we look outward, opening our hearts and speech that sometimes, the answers come from the least expected places and relief can be h ad.

Chapter 17

Breathing in

As I prepared to go lock up one of the businesses the other day my youngest daughter, Riyann, decided that she was tagging along. Why she decided to do so was beyond me, maybe she felt her old dad needed some help, maybe she just needed some time away from her sister, or better yet, maybe she just like the fact that dad liked to play his music loud and proud. Regardless of her reasoning, I welcomed the company. Her time with me, alone in the car, was not an uncommon sight. I've heard the child direct her elder sister on numerous occasions to ride with her mother because she needed her decompression time with dad. As she described, she uses the time to vent and discuss her day in a non-confrontational setting. I can tell you the child can definitely vent, ensuring that I am aware of her innermost feelings, without her sister or anyone else correcting her.

Upon entering the vehicle, and getting buckled in, Riyann turned to me and simply said "turn it up". Those words brought joy to my music loving soul and as I found her choice song on the radio, we began our journey down the hill. While driving, I noticed Riy was resting on the door frame, arms crossed below her chin, looking outwards, as the wind from the open window blew through her hair. Peering into the passenger side mirror I had a perfect view of my child as she relaxed, enjoying some modern music while she sucked in her surroundings. Seemingly carefree and not concerned over anything happening around her she remained in the position for the entire journey. With her eyes closed, the child face revealed a constant smile.

As we arrived at our destination, I thought about how Riyann's journey is different in many ways than her sisters and even my own. Being a self-prescribed protector of friends, youngest child, one who is committed to sharing kindness, all while possessing the traits of an introvert of sorts can take a toll on a girl. But at that moment, that time of calm, where she felt at ease, she had the opportunity to simply be still and breath in the greatness of nature and the things God has provided for us. It was then that she found solace through her solitude.

How different are we? Are we not like the child, the innocent? What a lesson we could learn from this nine-year-old child if we only take the time to listen. So often in life we get bogged down by everything going on around us. Whether it is work demands, education, family matters, or simply the hustle and bustle of life as we know it, we rarely take the time to close our eyes and simply breath, pondering the importance of a gentle breeze blowing in our face. Rather we carry on. We continue rushing from one place to another, rarely thinking about the impact our restless spirit is having upon not only ourselves but likewise on those around us, which we care about.

Watching my beloved child find that moment of calm reminded me of a passage I once read in the Scriptures "Be still and know that I am God". As my child found her point of calm, she experienced no worries stemming from outside influences. Riyann didn't have to worry about anything, she just took in the music along with nature, remaining still and breathing in life.

Life Lessons

Friends, take the necessary time to simply relax and breath in life. Close your eyes to the static this life can bring and just suck it all in, feeling the gentle breeze of calm, reviving you, and empowering you to carry on. For if you do, you too will experience a revived soul with a fresh outlook.

Chapter 18

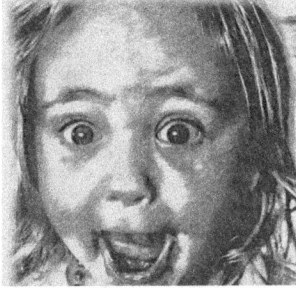

Making a Joyful Noise

While relaxing following a long, pretty much uneventful day, a year or so ago, my wife and I began conversing as we often do about our children. It was then that she enlightened me into what would become a point of comedy within our lives and a truly "Inside, unspoken" joke between she and I. As I begin to share our story, I would like to first state that I will not use names in this story. As A.E. Samaan once stated "the spoken word is ephemeral. The written word, eternal. A symphony, timeless". Hoping to share a little inspiration while simultaneously not wanting to bring my child any undue embarrassment, anonymity will be the best option and will surlily extend my existence in the event my beautiful child reads this.

As described, we were in deep thought when my wife revealed that our daughter, through her juvenile efforts, truly was a terrible singer. She described that she overheard both children singing and one was rather good but the second was not destined to be heard within that realm. She described that the child's effort was spot on, but her use of fluctuation and tone was absent and unfortunately unretrievable. Suffering from the same fate, I simply agreed considering my wife is as close to a professional singer as one can be. With a voice pure and angelic, the tones and smooth conversion of words to music is mesmerizing, a gift I have never obtained. For me, I have found myself destined to fantasizing about leading the band, singing and sending a message through song to countless others but never attempted to carry out the task for fear that everything within ear shot would surely suffer and the displeasure of many animals within hearing distance would simply we heard, long and loud.

Encouraging the child to find other avenues while, to be honest, lying to her about her abilities became the norm. As each year concludes, and the pending talent shows at school move closer, we move into damage control, trying our hardest to encourage her to engage in other options then showcasing her vocal abilities. Thus far we have been successful. With me for the most part forgetting about the topic I let my guard down. That as a mistake.

While relaxing, thinking of nothing but the current movie we were watching, my wife and I found ourselves alone while the children played downstairs in the rooms. Without notice, my phone rang with a notification of a pending message. Being unconcerned, I noticed that my child had sent me a video message. Upon opening it My little princess began explaining that she truly loved a poster she had on her wall and decided she wanted to sing it to me. Without further notice the child began singing the words. Sitting motionless, I experienced the unspeakable terror my wife spoke of previously. As her rendition of the written poem concluded, I looked at my wife in disbelief. Without notice, my child called me and asked me how I liked her song. Without hesitation I described that she did great, and I was glad she chose me to share it with. Cautioning her about allowing her friends to catch a glimpse of her greatness, she agreed she would hold off sending the video to others. Seeing the gleaming within her eyes as her father praised her brought me joy and validated her.

Life Lessons

As I consider this silly little story, I am reminded about the true enormity we as parents face, daily, as it pertains to our children. Although we would love to say that everything our children do is perfect and worthy of constant praise, our children are human and sometimes... it's just not that great. Therein lies true task of the father and mother. While encouraging our children for greatness, we must teach them that sometimes we have to just let go and do our best, then clothe ourselves in the reality that even though it's not the greatest it is ours. My child's voice will surely not win a contest, but you know what? It makes her feel good. It brings her joy, and truly that's alright. My job is simply to build her up with dignity while simultaneously doing our best to shape a workable, realistic, future for her.

Chapter 19

A Tough Lesson to Learn

I remember cringing as I heard my father say the words "this is going to hurt me more than it will you", as I prepared to be disciplined for whatever mischief I had been involved in that day. Those words always seemed ludicrous to me. How can it be that the one dealing out the discipline could feel worse than me, the one on the receiving end? It wasn't until I became a parent myself exactly what my father meant with those words. Just as the years helped me fully understand, this week's action by one of the girls helped her.

While we headed out to cross country practice Monday, Riyann informed me that she felt "kind of bad". Turning, I asked her why she felt bad, and she described that she was forced to give her little kitten a small "spankin" because she was being "really bad". She continued and drew a mental picture about how her kitten, Sky, had been picking on her sister, Mia. She said Sky jumped on her and began biting her head "real hard", so she was forced to intervene.

My attempts to lesson her burden through explaining that the kittens were probably just playing and that everything would be fine seemed to fall on deaf ears. As we continued traveling, I could hear Riyann talking to herself. She described, how she felt really bad and that she was sure her beloved kitten would now be mad at her or even worse stop loving her because of the spanking. After listening for a short time, I assured Riyann that everything would be fine between she and her kitten.

I explained that as a parent, we are forced at times to discipline our children. I assured her that we parents don't want to have to do it, but we must from time to time to ensure our children learn and remain safe. I explained that she just learned a valuable lesson about the true heart of a parent and how we at times must make unpopular decisions, which cause us pain, so our children can prosper. She stated she understood but remained rather solemn until we returned home, and her kitten welcomed her with her typical excitement filled romping only a kitten can do.

Life Lessons

Being forced to learn the tough lessons in life many times creates a moment of regret and angst about how those affected by our actions will view us moving past those lessons we teach. As with both me and my child, we have learned that decisions must be made, some which we truly don't want to make, but never- the -less, must be made to ensure a future of success for those we are tasked with bringing up. Does it hurt some? Absolutely. But through the internal pain we find that if we do it right, there awaiting our return, happy to see us, will be those special ones we truly care enough about to teach right from wrong.

Chapter 20

Safer Waters

While doing like many others did this past weekend, I tried my best to conquer the heat while sitting at the water's edge, celebrating our Independence Day. The day had been a whirlwind of chores and when the sun began to lower below the horizon the excitement of my little girls began to rise. Ensuring me that this year's fireworks display would be epic, the girls begged me to allow them to enjoy the show while doing a night swim at the pool. Although we rarely allow them to swim in the pool after dark, this year just seemed different.

Still not committing on the question of swimming in the pool or not I looked out and saw that instead of the normal, rowdy tourist group occupying the water I saw a large group of young children with their parents. Considering it a great opportunity for the girls to interact socially, I quickly let the girls know that their wish had been answered and they better hurry and get in the pool before the fireworks started. As you can imagine, sitting in the heat, watching my girls play in the water, was not on the top of my agenda for enjoyment. I would have much preferred to sit adjacent to the cool air flowing forth from my air conditioner. Deciding that the girl's enjoyment was more important than mine, I slowly moved to the pool side and found myself a chair to sit and watch the girls and the show.

As the girls made new friends, showing them their diving and swimming moves I battled the bugs which all who venture out on the beautiful, sweltering summer nights in Missouri undoubtedly understand. Placing a smile on my face, I did my best to find enjoyment while the girls had the time of their lives. As I watched the girls interacting with their new friends, I felt a joy in my soul that they have this awesome opportunity to meet new people daily, building friendships and experiences.

Throughout the night, some new families came to the pool, and some went. Each providing a new opportunity for the girls to "scope them out" and gingerly make their way over to them and make introductions. With the fireworks display in full motion I continued watching as the kid's excitement level grew. Approximately halfway through the display, I watched as a new family entered the pool area. The children did what children do best and all rapidly descended upon the water in the best manner possible, each choosing their own unique method of entry, sure to impress everyone watching.

As the older children all spread out in the pool I watched as a young child, affixed with multiple floaties on her arms remained playing, alone, in the shallow end. Within a short amount of time, I watched as the young child began moving a little bit further away from the shallows. As the child recognized that her feet no longer touched panic set in. flailing her arms, the child began asking for help, in a playful yet serious manner. I watched as no one seemed to recognize that the child was struggling. In a pool with multiple siblings and guardians no one came to the child's aid. Out of nowhere I watched as my daughter turned, recognizing that the child was scared, and swam over to her location. As my girl arrived, I could hear her ask, "are you ok?" as she placed her arms around the child.

Although I couldn't hear their interaction, I watched as my little girl held on to the child, swimming to the shallow end with the girl in tow. As they arrived at safer waters, the child's panic seemed to lift, and she remained with my girl. As the two sat in the shallow end, I listened as my child reassured the child that she was safe now. Not being satisfied that the child wouldn't venture to the deep again, my child remained with her, playing, and doing her best to keep the younger child safe.

A sense of pride flowed over me at that moment. I routinely have benefited from watching my children interact with others in kindness and compassion. This was no different. The only enhancement I felt throughout this situation was that I am eternally grateful to have had these two exceptional ladies in my life. For a young child to recognize the need and then to selfishly act upon that need is heartwarming.

Life Lessons

In a time and culture which seems to center upon our own wants and needs it was refreshing to see such a little child embrace the concept of lending a hand as a need arises. In my little life saver, I see the person I hope to become. A caring and compassionate individual who is willing to place my own fun and enjoyment on the back burner to help others, leading them by the hand to safer waters. Reach out a hand my friends.

Chapter 21

A Refusal to Give Up

T hroughout the winter months, Lilli, my ten-year-old daughter, has continued along her path of striving to become a better cross-country runner. Although I remain bewildered at the thought that people truly enjoy this sport, I have come accustomed to doing everything in my power to encourage my child and set her up for success. As we discussed the perfect training regiment, designed to make her a top-notch runner and athlete, Lilli voiced her desire to begin training on the steep hills of Skyline Drive in Carter County. Thinking to myself that this child would never be able to consistently train on the brutal environment I outwardly agreed that the course would enhance her abilities while inwardly chuckling a little bit at the thought of how this child will soon experience the full wrath of trying to run over a mountain.

Over the next few months, I watched as my child quickly displayed a determination I truly failed to recognize before that point. The child listened to guidance and before long she was running the course with little discomfort and even fewer stopping points. The entire regiment of getting in the car, turning up the air conditioner, and activating the vehicles hazard lights became tiresome, yet routine as the child stated she was ready to train and ol dad put a smile on his face, ensuring that his daughter knew he would sacrifice a little time to ensure her safety. As we prepared for the run this week something new happened. As Lilli stretched, her younger sister, Riyann stated her desire to run alongside her sister.

To gain a full glimpse of what transpired one must understand that Riyann and Lilli differ drastically in their qualities and strengths. Where Lilli is determined to excel academically and hates coming in second to anyone let alone her sister, Riyann is content hanging out, smelling the roses, and watching the wind blow, both are exceptional in their own way. On this day, Riyann was determined to tag along. Graciously, the older sibling agreed and encouraged her sister.

As the two started out, both performed well, remaining stride for stride with each other, both seemingly enjoying not only the fresh air of spring, but the competition brough about by the younger child engaging. As the curse moved into the predominantly uphill stage I observed as the younger sibling began to tire. Undoubtedly the tiredness stemmed from her lack of prior running in that manner or quite possibly her getting over the fun of running alongside her sister. I watched as she began stopping more often, attempting to mask her pure, unrelenting, exhaustion with simple gestures of picking flowers from the shoulder of the roadway. Recognizing her plight, I pulled up alongside her and told her she could get in the car if she wanted. Striving to help the child maintain her pride, I explained that she did well and considering it was her first-time running skyline, she should be proud, but could rest.

The child looked up to me, and quickly said, "nope, I have to finish with Lilli", then turned and began running again. Although the act of actually running became simply a matter of a few steps at a time, the child persisted, trailing her elder sister as she ran. As I watched through the windshield, I could feel the burn which was taking place in the child's legs and recognized the sharp pain piercing her sides. never less, she continued her course, thwarting several efforts by me to get her to give up and simply relax in the vehicle. Each time describing that she had to finish with her sister.

As we reached the final quarter mile I began conspiring with Lilli. Describing that her sister was hurting since it was her first time, Lilli and I decided that we would forego the final segment. As Lilli described to Riyann that the run was done for the day, I noticed something quite interesting. Riyann knew better. As Lilli attempted to shield her sister from any further pain Riyann simply turned, said, no, we must finish the course, and began running again. Lilli quickly followed suite and the two children completed their two-mile run over hills and through valleys with their good old dad in tow.

The child and her self-described "jelly legs" entered the house where she proudly told her mother that her legs no longer worked, and she though she may not survive but had helped her sister finish the race. Watching the child, I found an entirely new level of appreciation and pride as her father. Her perseverance and unwillingness to take the easy road reveled a side of her we had not seen.

Life Lessons

The thought of how in life we face what seems like the unsurmountable tasks or mountains placed in our path flashed across my mind. Riyann displayed through her actions that our successful maneuvering through those difficult and seemingly unachievable moments many times depends upon our ability to remain persistent and never give up. Today a nine-year-old child taught me that only through a full commitment and desire to overcome all the temporary pain and suffering which comes along with success, can we achieve the greatness we are. Run strong my friends, keeping the finish line in sight while taking a moment to enjoy the flowers along the way.

Chapter 22

An Inconvenient Nest

A natural biproduct of purchasing older buildings to renovate and turn them into something the family can be proud of is seemingly the never-ending supply of wild birds. When our family began the process of cleaning up an older roadside motel, we were shocked at the mere number of birds which had decided to call the eves, trees, and wires attached to the building their home. In a symbolic form of resistance, each of our attempts to repair the holes, or scare off the flock brought with it an epic battle of sorts, with the birds making it evident that their claim would be fought for and if we were going to succeed in removing them, we would surely know they were there and have a story to tell.

I recall the year we boarded up all the holes, created by the birds. For one day, I stood with pride, gazing upon the bird free creation I had made and sighed a sigh of relief that those destructive creatures were gone. As I looked closer, in the distance, I saw a sight which would truly strike fear in any human's soul. Surrounding the property, perched upon the power lines were seemingly hundreds of birds peering intently, downward, upon me like warriors preparing for a secondary offensive. Quietly, yet stealthily I decided that it was time to go inside to ensure I was not the leading character in a birds two saga, made for television.

Interestingly enough, the birds did carry out their seminally horrid plan on retaliation the following day. As I left the building, I noticed that the ground surrounding a large oak tree stationed directly outside the office doorway, was rattled with remnants of bird biproducts and the tree was full of the little critters, all screeching warnings, or laughing with each other, as I dodged the gifts they sent from above. Over time, the mess was cleared up and the birds simply moved back to the rear of the property creating new holes to perch upon.

Last Summer, my beautiful wife decided that a certain hanging plant caught her eye and would look great directly outside the office door. Agreeing, I went about the task of hanging the plant, taking a moment to admire my handiwork once I was done. The next day I simply had to laugh as I walked outside and noticed that overnight, a bird had erected a fully functional nest deep within the confines of my wife's prided hanging plan. Later that day, as I showed her the nest, we observed that a single blue egg lay in the nest. Then two, three, and finally four eggs. Not being happy about the nest, my wife quickly decided that even though she didn't like the idea of it being there, the fact that eggs were present would ensure the nests existence at least for one year.

The little nest proved to be a true-life lesson for our family and guests of the motel. As the girls, Leona, and I watched the life cycle of the birds we found great enjoyment. Likewise, the nest and its inhabitants became a visual reminder of how the little things in life can bring a smile to faces and even soften the heart of the biggest, gruffest men when watching babies grow. Our guests loved the birds as did we and we quickly forgot about our earlier battles, centering on the joy of life.

Life Lessons

Today a mural hangs in the office which depicts the life and growth of our little bird babies. A constant reminder that sometimes our sacrifices, in the end, add joy to not only us personally but likewise to those who are joining us through this journey called life. Understanding that through battles we can find solace is a key to carrying on, as we experience things which initial may seem to be negative but end up teaching us the true value of life.

Chapter 23

A Friend indeed

Wondering what was taking so long, I began to feel my anxiety rise. Our girls have begun adding responsibilities to their lives through implementing chores into their daily routines. One of the dreaded chores for both girls is the daily trek from the house to the dumpster, which lies up the driveway, near the roadway, to dispose of the days trash. This past week I reminded Riyann, and she headed out in her normal manner, smiling all the way. Full trash bag in tow, she began the arduous (to a nine-year-old) journey. As time passed, I began to realize she was taking a bit longer than normal.

Fearing the worst, something I many times do, I quickly sprang from my seat and walked over to the front door to check on my little adventurer. Expecting to find her playing with the latest leaf or rock she came across or possibly the neighborhood stray cat, I peered out the glass window and to my surprise I didn't see her. She wasn't standing by the road waving an adorable hello to passing motorists like she often did and wasn't doing her best to simply be herself in her own special way, she was nowhere to be found.

As my heart dropped, I opened the door and stepped outside. Preparing myself for every parent's worst nightmare, Immediately, I noticed some movement to my left. I felt a wave of relief flow across me as I observed Riyann making her way through the wooded area between our home and the neighbors. With a look like a startled animal, Riy saw me and with a big smile on her face yelled "my neighbor friend is home". Knowing that she was safe, I simply responded with a hearty ok and stood watching as she made her way over to her friends front door.

Our neighbors, Riy's good friends, had just arrived home from a trip where they had been visiting some close family members out of state. Little did they know that the opportunity to see their children and grandchildren over the holidays would soon be overshadowed by the fact that Riyann would surely drill them about every aspect of their trip and pressure them to get some gardening done, a chore she had fully bought into whenever she saw them working their flower garden. Never waiting for an invitation, she would see them outside, walk over, and simply jump right in and begin helping, taking in the tutelage from some truly good people.

Upon assuring that everything was alright, I listened as Riy welcomed them home and as I feared, began quizzing them on why they had been gone so long. As good people often do, our neighbors cheerfully welcomed the child and appeased her curiosity. Later, Lilli inquired where her sister was and upon hearing that she was welcoming the neighbors back home she hurriedly sprung out the door and headed over. Checking on the girls, I later found them standing beside their friend, learning the proper art of planting flowers, while Lilli lectured Riyann about making sure that mom and dad knows where she is before leaving the yard.

Life Lessons

While I sat, content that my babies were safe, the thought about how lucky we are crossed my mind. Seldom are we able to enjoy the presence of others who truly care for knowledge. My hope is that each of us will slow down a little this year and enjoy the company of those around us. Seek out the wisdom my friends while allowing not only ourselves but our younger generation to truly benefit from being in the presence of those who have lived a bit longer and have an abundance of knowledge to impart and may we always see children as an opportunity to teach rather than an obstacle. Be a good neighbor my friends.

Chapter 24

Hang On

A s I picked my children up from school the other day it was evident that my one of the girls had, had a bad day. Although not voicing her frustration or what had gone wrong, she simply sat in the back seat of the car, somber, sad faced and quiet. Understanding over the years that it was far more effective, and self-preserving to simply let it be, remaining quiet as she told me everything was fine, I simply told her if she needed to talk her mom and I were here for her. After a short time, and I must admit, a bit of prodding from me, the child broke her silence explaining that some of her friends had been giving her a hard time about things which seemed silly to good old dad but were life altering to a child of ten.

Following listening to the child's plight and after giving her a little pep talk about not giving up and remaining true to herself, I began doing what has got me in a moderate amount of trouble with her mother; I began giving her strategies to cope with the mean children she encounters. Realizing, the last time she and I discussed strategies, I ended up being pulled aside by my awesome wife, warning me about my "master class on dealing with confrontation" due to the child's following through with my suggestions and leaving several other children bewildered by her reaction and response to their teasing, to say it mildly, I stopped in my tracks. Not wanting the child to again, misinterpret what dad may jokingly say, then repeat it, I simply reiterated her awesomeness and the importance of not allowing what others say get to her.

As the evenings mood changed and she was back to her normal self, I thought about a moment many years prior which found myself and my eldest daughter at our church in Colorado. As I went to the nursery to retrieve my two-year-old, she decided that it was an opportune time to seat herself on the top of my right foot and hold on to my lower leg with a tight grip, reminiscent of a vise grip, refusing to release. Deciding that removing the child would most likely bring with it a moderate amount of screaming, and why not let the kid have some fun, I simply began my journey back to my office, along the back of the sanctuary, with my child in tow, like a unremovable growth affixed to my leg.

As I began my journey, my daughter giggled with delight over her newly found carnival ride. Struggling to keep my balance, I quietly traversed the back of the sanctuary, striving ever so quietly to make it to the other side without disrupting the choir practice taking place. As I made it successfully to the mid-way point of the sanctuary, I was feeling pretty good about myself. Not only did I show my strength to my child, but I also added to her joy and was not disruptive. That's what I thought, at least. Without warning, I began hearing light laughter. As the tone of laughter began rising, I turned my head towards the choir to see what had happened. It was then that I realized, my attempts to make it across the sanctuary unnoticed was a complete failure as the watering eyes of the choir members revealed their pleasure in watching me and my child.

Life Lessons

As we engage life, we come across events and people who for whatever reason, simply, have a negative outlook or derive pleasure from trying to bring us down. Understanding why people act in such a manner is many times pointless. Their mean spirited and negative behavior can many times leave us frustrated or angry, intern causing us to change our outlook on events, people, or even life. When we are confronted with these situations, we must simply grab hold of the positive and hold on, being true to ourselves, allowing no one or nothing to lower our level of compassion. As my child did, grabbing hold and failing to let go of the enjoyable things in life, will not only firm up our individual worth but likewise enhance the journey of others. Hold tight friends, giggle, and enjoy the moment.

Chapter 25

Knowing your worth

As I sat, enjoying a quiet evening at home, the sounds of children playing pierced the silence. Shortly after the loss of two of our family's beloved pet cats, Leona and I gave in an allowed the girls to adopt two energetic farm kittens. The squeals of joy emendated throughout the entire house as the girls entered their third week of motherhood for their little furry babies. Quickly transitioning from the bedroom area to the living room the girls began describing the latest antic the kittens had done, assuring us that the babies were simply the most precious things alive.

As I listened intently, happy that the girls were able to find joy in our newest family members, Leona began joking about how at one time, while she was young, she had accumulated a rather large heard of outside cats, to her father's dismay. Why the multitude of furry little beasts routinely followed her home and decided to encamp under their porch was truly the question for the ages according to Leona, as she flashed a Cheshire like grin on her face. She eventually broke down and admitted to the girls that she would routinely walk around as she played and when she came across an old, raggedy cat, she would fall in love and begin playing with it. Her deep love and compassion for those strays caused her to ensure their needs were met, although secretly, by placing ample amounts of food out for them. The interaction would eventually end up at her home where she continued to care for the small animals, ensuring that they knew they were loved by one little girls from Louisiana.

As Leona relayed this childhood story to the girls, I couldn't help but draw several inferences to how this beautiful, intelligent woman's childhood experiences had inadvertently transferred onto her children. That or simply said, children are simply much more accepting, attentive, and visionaries then most adults are. I thought about all the cats which have innocently wandered onto the motel property. Assuredly, only wishing to find a meal, do a little exploring, or see what was going on, only to be swooped up by one of my beautiful children, forever having their lives altered for the good by someone who fell in love with them.

Life Lesson

Thinking about the joy the girls derive from their kittens and their deeply instilled desire to care for animals, my mind instantly thought about how it is important to remember that we should never let anyone tell us or treat us like we are not worth full price. Within each of us lies value. Regardless of whether we are rich or not so well off, strong or weak, frazzled because of life or right where we need to be, we have worth and deserve to be treated as such. As with the stray cats, each of us need a friend, someone who will swoop them up and simply show that they care and are willing to understand.

Take a moment to explore all the good that lays around us friends, be willing to see beyond the outward appearance and into the true heart of others. For when we look beyond the dirt and rubble, it is then that we may just find a gem meant just for us.

Chapter 26

Welcoming Outreached Arms

W hile seated in the congregation, several years ago, listing to a Sunday sermon from my pastor, my child was having a difficult time concentrating. As I carried out my routine fatherly duties of attempting to keep my children focused on learning and not hampering other people's worship my youngest child moved to a position in front of me. She quickly asked me to braid her hair and considering the alternative of pure utter disruption I gladly agreed.

As we all grow older, we take on certain traits and characteristics which we have learned along the way. One such trait I was blessed to learn is the ability to French braid hair. Although many times, when speaking of my ability to others I've been faced with skepticism and a moderate amount of disbelief, I've enjoyed the time it allows with my bonding with my daughters. I remain thankful that a friend, I knew the second year I was in the Navy took it upon herself to teach me not only how to French braid but likewise how to braid correctly. Little did I know back then just how useful it would become.

As any good parent would, given the opportunity to engage their children while keeping them from making a scene, I quickly positioned my daughter in front of me as we gazed forward, listening to the Pastor share his Godly wisdom. While I worked my magic with the strands of her shoulder length brown hair, I remained fixated on the words of the sermon. Spinning the portions of hair this way and the next that way, over sections of hair and some under, I quickly completed my task and must say it looked good. With each braid perfectly in place, from a father's point of view, I shifted my glance from the Pastor to my child and felt a momentary sense of pride over how great the braid turned out.

As I held the lower portion of her hair, I realized that although I had truly completed the perfect trifecta of fatherhood, worshiping through the sermon while braiding my kid's hair and better yet, I kept her occupied, I experienced a fast evolving "oh crud" moment. What I had failed to recognize when my child asked me to braid her hair was, we had no band to keep the braid in place. I quickly glanced towards her sister to see if she had an extra band around her wrist and asked my child if she had one. As the clock seemed to slow considerably, I'm pretty sure the anxiety level rose to levels higher than they should have as I searched for any item, I could use to tie off the small locks of hair and preserve this fatherly masterpiece.

It was then that I received the surprise I was not expecting. Out of nowhere and from multiple directions, the arms of several mothers and older daughters reached out towards me, each grasping a hair tie in their hand. Somewhat shocked, I gladly grasp one band and quietly thanked the kind lady who became the provider. What I had failed to observe was that while I was going about my business of listening to the sermon and doing my best to keep my child from disrupting the service, I in fact had become the focal point of several ladies within the congregation. My attempt to keep my child quiet had in fact drawn the attention of others and provided the comical relief they needed. Later, several of those ladies approached me and described how they were captivated by the fact that I knew how to French braid hair, you see I'm a burly, big guy which no one would believe I could interact in such a manner and secondly, that I would so openly be willing to engage my child in such a manner.

Life Lessons

As I thought about this encounter, I am reminded about just how often we do our best to accomplish tasks without realizing that the tools we require aren't always within us. At times, our best of intentions leaves us in a position where we must be able to recognize the outreached hands of assistance and be willing to take hold, so our goals and dreams can be realized. Although we all would like to believe we can do it on our own, it is through a brotherhood and sisterhood, a community with outreached arms, that our true vision can become a reality. Welcome the outreached hands, for we never know when our actions will not only help us but also become the means by which another finds contentment.

Chapter 27

The Power of Influence

My peaceful Labor Day was shattered as my child emerged from her bedroom. With the intent to simply relax and have no duties or responsibilities for this one day I had planned on catching up on the latest Netflix series, moving very little, and for all practical purposes blending in until it was my time to light up the barbeque and fulfill my time-honored duty of making the perfect dinner in accordance to Labor Day tradition. As my child walked into the living room, she voiced her desire to go out and do some running to prepare for this week's cross-country meet.

Although content laying on the couch, I was faced with a battle of will deep within my mind. Do I continue in my present course of action and cement my position on the couch, or do I follow through and escort my daughter while she follows my earlier advice about the importance of remaining committed to a strict training regiment, designed to enhance her abilities athletically?

You guessed it, without hesitation, I rose from my perch and off we went. Now don't get me wrong, running was not on my agenda this day nor any other in the foreseeable future. Those days have passed and are many years and multiple pounds separated from the good ol days and now. My contribution is to sit in an air-conditioned car following my child to ensure her safety while she beats and batters her body in the name of success. This run was not like any other in the recent past. She began by describing that she was pretty sure she was going to tackle the two- mile course and as I outwardly voiced my approval, inwardly I was certain my child had lost her ever loving mind.

The run was relatively uneventful with the occasional vehicle cautiously passing us along the roadway. As Lilli ran, I was impressed at how well she was doing considering the high humidity and to be honest, her lack of tackling the brutal course previously. As we approached the halfway point, which happened to be at the top of a steep incline, Lilli grabbed a quick drink of water and informed me that she had decided she was only going to conquer the mile and a half portion of the course this time out. Agreeing, I shared my excitement about how great she was doing and encouraged her to finish strong. As she began the final stretch of her practice, I saw something interesting.

As Lilli struggled on, I observed a vehicle approaching me from behind. It was evident the vehicle saw my hazard lights as they began slowing down. After a short distance, I watched as the vehicle cautiously began passing me. As the vehicle passed me, adjacent to my child, my super dad senses moved into full action mode. I sat up in my seat, as I watched the rear window begin to lower as it approached my child. Within seconds I saw a petite hand extend outward from the vehicle, displaying a thumbs up. I watched Lilli nod her head as the vehicle passed her by. The interaction seemed to have a motivating effect on Lilli. I watched as she passed up the finish line and continued along the full two-mile course.

Upon finishing, I asked her what the passengers in the white vehicle said to her and she replied that the high school students simply said she was doing great and to finish strong and not to give up. She described how those words encouraged her to continue and to not stop short of her original goal. Upon hearing this, my faith in the human soul was refreshed. So many times, we in the older generation fail to recognize the power and influence our younger people have. This simple expression of community, shown by those students depicted in my mind the power of influence and mentorship.

So many times, we get caught up in ourselves that we neglect our sense of community and the benefit we can provide for others. In my opinion the simple act, by these young people, of rolling down a window displaying a positive gesture and sharing a few simple words of encouragement to a stranger who happened to be much younger and very impressionable, was the ultimate example of leadership. True leadership results when those in a position of power are concerned little about their selves and more about ensuring that those below them are equipped with the tools necessary to carry on in their absence.

These young people truly are leaders and should be proud of their legacy. For to take a moment to cheer on a child creates no harm but rather a potential lifetime of success, commitment, and resilience, all because of your simple act of compassion.

Life Lessons

Step outside the norm my friends and shout out those words of encouragement. You never know who may see or hear your words and the impact your influence will have on their lives.

Chapter 28

Reversing the Roles

As the sun rose above the horizon this morning it was apparent that the new day brought with it a moderate amount of stress spilling forth from not only the holiday season but likewise the normal day to day responsibilities, we as parents feel. My wife was especially feeling the frustrations of everything piling on and found it difficult to get motivated after a sleepless night. As she and I spoke, little did I know that our children were also paying attention. The conversation which ensued was not only heartwarming but also day altering.

Following a brief break in our conversation I observed as my daughters began strategically moving into position around their mother. As I set back and began finishing up my personal preparations my daughter moved adjacent to her mother and began explaining that we couldn't lose sight of the important things in life. She described that what other people thought of us was not all that important because the only "important thing is what we think about ourselves". She then went on to describe to her mother "so don't stress about it at all." Explaining that sometimes people treat us badly because they don't have a heart for other people... and they might be on "the naughty list because of their heart" for treating people badly. Both children then reassured their mother that everything would be alright and to welcome this day because it was going to be a good day.

As I watched the interaction between mother and child, I was stricken with not only an inability to speak but also a deep pride stemming from the manner by which true kindness and compassion for another human flowed forth from the lips of my two beautiful daughters. Although mere children, eight and nine years old, the words spewing forth from their mouths were comparable to ages of combined wisdom. As I watched, I thought about how these two little gifts chose to do everything in their power to change the outlook of a beloved friend. Likewise, allowing those around us to lift us up and help us to regain course is imperative. Although their mother, later, voiced her embarrassment that her children saw her frustrated, she appreciated the true compassion they showed.

Life Lesson

So often we observe others in a state of crisis and have not only the ability but also the opportunity to effect positive change. The thing is will we. Will we take the risk to meet others at their place of need, stripping ourselves of all our self-erected defense mechanisms, bearing our soul to lessen another's burden? When we do, as a humble eight-year-old proved, it is then that we can truly pass on the wisdom we have learned throughout history and maybe just lighten the burden of another in the process. Reach forth my friends and grasp the hands which have been extended in compassion, when your surroundings are brighter, share that same hand with another in an attempt to lighten the load of another.

Chapter 29

Unlikely Hero's

As I watched the girl's nit-pick each other the other day, finding fault in the mere fact that their sibling consumed air, I got a little tickled. Trying my best to hold back my laughter, I watched as one child would voice her disdain for the actions or words of her sister while the other quickly countered with evidence of her own why her sister needed to shape up. The fact that good old dad would interject his words of wisdom relating to the benefits of sisters, family and having the back of our siblings fell upon deaf ears as I was simply as a noise in the breeze to the little combatants. As the battle raged, I found that it took all I had not to record their conversation for future use in a well-planned out black mail scheme. As the girls either tired of the combat or simply became reserved to the fact that the other was being unreasonable, I found the perfect moment to interject.

Forgetting that trying to rationalize with an angry nine- and ten-year-old, fresh out of battle, was pointless, I began discussing the importance of communication and compromise. As you can imagine my attempts to turn the battle into a teaching moment was enormously unsuccessful and met with the occasional "she did" and She said". Deciding that the only plausible solution was a bit of time apart, I directed the girls to go play in their rooms, adding the necessary parental phrase, we have all come to love and adore "and

I better not hear any more arguing". As the girls stomped to their perspective rooms, I reminded myself just how lucky I was to be blessed with the girls, even thru the conflicts.

As the silence of the sibling cease fire continued, I began thinking about how the same two children, entrenched in battle, failing to give in, and determined to win truly could turn the proverbial page and have each other's back when necessary. My thoughts flowed to several years prior where my youngest child was promoted to a grade level where she attended the same school building as her older sibling. Silently listening as her older sibling talked to her mother and I about a male classmate who had consistently treated her poorly, even resorting to physically assaulting the child. The younger child simply listened. As her sister revealed that the boy had began treating her friends poorly, she voiced her concern that he would again begin "being mean" to her. Her mother and I, and the child devised an adequate strategy for addressing the bully while her sister continued to sit idly by, seemingly not paying attention. It wasn't until approximately one week later that we realized the younger child wasn't simply ignoring her sister but developing a strategy of her own.

While at home eating dinner, as was routine with our family, we asked the girls how their day went. With excitement gleaming, Lilli began describing to us that while on the playground, the boy began picking on one of her friends. Feeling frustrated that she was unable to protect her friend she described she didn't know what to do. It was then, as Lilli described, that she saw movement from her side. Without noticed, she watched as her little sister ran up and addressed the situation by throwing the boy to the ground, standing over him while she told him he better not hurt her sister or her friends again. Shocked by the child's actions, I must admit, I felt pride in the fact that the child solved the problem for her sister. I thanked Riy for her help but warned that she should speak to the teachers rather than resorting to physical violence. Her reply was both revealing and humorous. She simply described that when the teachers won't do anything sometimes sisters have to have each other's backs and do what's necessary".

Life Lessons

The situation reminded me that life involves moments where our heroes are not only those, we rely upon but also sometimes come from the most unexpected places. We all have strengths which are many times on full display for others to see, what we many times try to forget is that likewise, we are also weak in one area or another. It is through community and a willingness to be on the lookout for others, interceding, when necessary, that we all can fulfill our destiny and make it through this life unscathed. Be someone's hero this week my friends.

Chapter 30

Smuggling Candy

As I begin our story, I must be careful with my words, to ensure all unnamed little people continue reaping the rewards of what we are about to talk about. Becoming aware on one of my children's recent antics, I simply couldn't resist sharing them with you. Yesterday, while preparing to go home for the evening Riyann, my nine-year-old, hurriedly got in my vehicle, choosing to ride with good ol dad rather than her momma. As we went about our normal routine of ensuring we were seat belted in, hadn't forgotten anything important like her iPad or other devices, and were set for a relaxing time at home, I began pulling out of the parking space.

As I placed the vehicle in reverse, I felt a gentle nudge on my elbow. Turning my head in the direction of the nudge, I observed Riyann looking upward. What caught my eye at that moment would leave me unable to fully contain my inner laughter at the pure, unrestrained, honesty of the child. The easiest way to describe what transpired is to attempt to help you understand through talking about what it looked like.

Similar to a street level drug deal we have all seen go down on the television screen. You know, the one with one person looking at another while the person, attempting to unload the product shyly looks around, then nodding in the direction of their hand which is closely held to their side, hoping to not draw attention. That is what I saw. As I looked down, genuinely saying to myself "what on earth is this child doing" I observed what can be widely considered every parent's worst nightmare. Ok, maybe not the worst, but definitely one which ranks rather high on the "oh no" list.

In my child's hand lay a large sized, zip lock baggie, wrapped securely around two large crunch, chocolate candy bars. As I attempted to nod with the proverbial "nice" ... response, Riy's eyes quickly darted to the right, and apparently observing something or someone, her hand rushed to return the treasured package back within the deep confines of her backpack. Before I could say anything, she described that her friend was upset because she (Riy) forgot to bring her candy today, but she was prepared for tomorrow.

Being worried that my child may have fallen victim to the school yard bully requiring payment in the form of candy, I inquired as to why her friend wanted her to provide her with "goodies". Riy quickly and quite decisively described that she had a really good friend, whose mom "is pretty rude". As a point of reference, When Riyann calls someone rude it is normally because they are setting rules or enforcing them. She went on to say that she supplies her friend with candy, daily, because her mom won't. She stated her giving the friend candy makes her happy and allows her to enjoy the better things in life. She asked if her supply was adequate and acceptable. What could a dad say, you guessed it, I said it surely was.

As you can imagine, the remainder of our journey home consisted with an inward struggle for me. One side, the dad side, truly thought the entire interaction, hidden gift, and reasoning was humorous. The other part of me, the parental side, cautioned her against going against the child's mothers wishes because there may be a valid reason for her restrictive diet. Although saying she understood, I'm relatively certain the transaction involving the ever so yummy treats moved forward. So now, I realize, I'm the father of the local candy smuggler, not absent compassion, as she attempts to meet the sugar high needs of another nine-year-old.

Life Lessons

In life it seems that the moments which catch us off guard can at times bring us a needed level of humor as well as thought invoking consideration about how the manner, we choose to engage compassion and kindness sometimes goes against the norm while maintain the ultimate goal of supplying a need. We must be ever mindful of possibilities as we develop ways to share with others.

Chapter 31

Showing No Fear

I grinned as I watched Lilli seated on the couch covering her eyes in terror as she anticipated the next scene from the movie she and her mother were watching. Her desire to be an active participant in her mothers' adventures led her to take part even when her comfort level wasn't the highest. Both Lilli and Riyann have found enjoyment from their mother's occasional horror flick binging and although they would never admit it, have fought off their own fears while ensuring their mother that they could hang along with her. Ensuring that they realized what they were watching was purely Hollywood and not real life, the entire situation and aftermath has been the sounding board for several unique conversations as you could imagine.

On this particular day, Momma had decided to follow through with her child's request to find a scary movie to watch. Upon hearing the discussion, I quickly learned that Lilli didn't want to watch just any scary movie she wanted to watch the ultimate movie which would remain etched in her mind for "a good time". As I sat, I kicked up my feet, leaned back, and prepared to enjoy the pending disaster which would surely unfold within my little family. Grinning, my lovely wife looked at me with a seemingly Cheshire grin, fully understanding what soon would transpire.

As we began watching the show, I recall thinking to myself that although simplistic in nature, the show had a couple scenes which could be considered scary. You know, the lone doll, holding the memories of past generations, ultimately deciding to unleash its fury upon a new family, simply because they dared to move into a new house. Purely unrealistic yet fun for a parent watching his child follow through with her desire to watch a scary show. I must admit, understanding that every dad has a responsibility to ensure their children were engaged, I full-filled that responsibility. As the room drew quiet, the timing was perfect. Being unable to take it any longer I let out a loud scream, sending the children scurrying elsewhere soon to return, laughing because dad scared the dickens out of them.

Believing that their mother and I had failed, I mentioned to my loving wife that we could find a better, scarier movie to watch if the girls wanted. Without hesitation, Lilli ensured us that the movie was fine, and she believed she had something else to do in her room. The next few days consisted of a rapid removal, from their rooms, of any dolls similar in nature to the one depicted in the show and a constant need to remain tethered to their sister's side. Our thinking that the movie cured the girls from wanting to take part in mommas movie choices was short lived and off base as the following week was a repeat with the girls begging to have a family "scary movie" night.

Since that fateful night, our family has come to enjoy our goofy "scary movie nights". Although we pre-screen the titles we show the girls, we strive to feed their desire to a point and dad continues to find ample moments of being able to interject a horrid scream, terrible acting, or simple attempt to add to the ambiance of our girls' adventure. The entire adventure has taught me that persistence and striving to overcome our own personal fears in order to fit in, is not necessarily bad at times.

Life Lessons

Having a full understanding of when fitting in is beneficial or even productive can be overshadowed by our inability to understand that there are times when it's likewise ok to not engage. Life is a series of choices, all with ramifications, some positive and some not so much so. Our ability to take risks, show vulnerability, and overcome fear is the framework by which we can find a new level of fulfillment and earn wisdom along the way.

Chapter 32

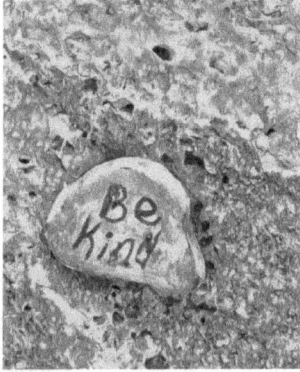

Influencing Action

I remember, many years ago, learning about how our actions are important and many times influence the actions of others. I never really gave the concept much thought but centered myself on an ideal my parents consistently reiterated with me, the value of doing good and doing it for the right reasons. As I have grown into adulthood, the attempts at fair play and being the better person dominated my behavior, although just like everyone else I've faltered at times, falling short of my goals, harboring frustrations and ill will momentarily. This past week brought the concept back to light in its full glory as I returned home from work.

Upon completing work, I drove to our motel, where my children were hanging out with their grandmother. As I opened the door, I was greeted by my child, bearing a smile, as she moved quickly throughout the kitchen. Sensing that the child wanted to disclose some valuable truth to me, I inquired as to how her day had been. Without hesitation, the child described how she learned that one of our motel guests had children. She went on to describe that her grandmother had told her that the children may need a friend to play with because their family was going through a difficult time in their lives. She went on to describe that she heard they had very little clothing and were really struggling.

As we spoke about the situation my daughter began telling me how she felt bad for her new friends, and she felt it was necessary to do something about it. My child described that she hoped I wasn't upset, but she had gone to her room and collected six (6) sets of tops and bottoms which no longer fit her. She described she made sure the outfits were nice and matched, and she gave the clothing to the children, hoping "it would make them happier". As I listened to the child rationalize her decision and actions I simply sat in silence. Looking up to me with wide eyes and hopeful heart, she asked if I was upset.

As I looked at the child, I reassured her that I felt her behavior was awesome and I was happy that she chose to give of herself to help another. We spoke about how sometimes others go through valleys in their lives, just like we can, and being the means by which others can prosper is admirable and the right thing to do. Expecting nothing in return was the key, I explained. As we went about our routine duties I will admit, I fought back to urge to inquire more fully as to the child's motives and how she went about the process of choosing the perfect outfits, but simply let it go. Instead, I simply enjoyed the moment and thought about how truly awesome and kind my children were.

I thought about how truly gifted we are as humans, when we are able to recognize a need within others and then, without any need of public recognition, act accordingly to lessen the burden. Being rich or poor, status driven or a recluse, has little bearing on our actions and choices. Rather, when we choose to help another through their difficulties, hoping for nothing more than their progress, it is then that we recognize that our actions truly can have an impact.

My child felt compassion and in the end, pride for her ability to recognize a need and acting upon that need. A pride which is shared by her father as he watches his child seek not the attention from service but rather the results of their action, and the betterment of another's journey.

Life Lessons

In a world where seemingly, everyone strives to be an influencer let us not forgot our children are watching and whether we like it or not, they mirror our actions, words, and our very choices. Choose actions wisely my friends, for there is an entire generation which will someday emulate what they learn today. Give them a show, future generations will be proud of.

Chapter 33

Fears of a Father

As excitement filled the air, I watched while my girls crawled into the car after their first cheerleading camp practice. My desire to inquire as to how everything went was overshadowed by both girl's constant chatter about how "cool" and helpful, the older cheerleaders were and how they not only had a great time learning, but also learned a great deal. The girls continued describing to me and their mother, about everything which transpired, barely containing the enormous amount of excitement which resulted from attending. As a father I was excited not only for them but with them... well at least, up to the point that they described their positions on the newly developed cheerleading team.

Through her constant chatter, Riyann began describing that both she and her sister had secured the much desired "flier" positions within the team. As Lilli began explaining that the team consists of two primary positions, the flier, and the base positions. My mouth immediately voiced my approval and excitement for their accomplishment as I noticed my mind begin processing the words which came out of their mouths. Without hesitation, my mind immediately rebooted. The reboot came rapidly as with the lowering of an iron clad, medieval gate, slamming to the ground as a means of protecting those inside. The only words I could effectively say, with a smiling face, to ensure my concern did not become apparent, were "did you say you are fliers?"

As the girls again, happily, explained that the flier position was "big" and they were both so proud to have been chosen since they would be the team member who is thrown into the air and at times, the top of the cheerleader pyramid. Fighting back my initial inclination to say "oh heck no" I continued voicing my excitement for them and their accomplishment. As the words of approval spilled forth from my lips, I held back my fatherly concern over not only one, but both, of my daughters being the one child who is thrust into the air while their fellow nine- and ten-year-old classmates are tasked with catching them. As visions of broken bones, bumps and bruises readily flowed through my mind like a 1920's silent movie, I decided that good old dad shouldn't rain on their proverbial parade of happiness but rather be as supportive as possible, hoping only that their love for the sport was short lived.

Anyone who has been blessed with the opportunity to welcome a child into their life, fully understands the difficulty of releasing the reigns somewhat. I remember several years prior as my eldest child entered her junior year in high school, I had to come to the realization that although protecting her was an imperative part of fatherhood, likewise was allowing her to experience life and being allowed to make more and more decisions with each passing day, sometimes resulting in mistakes, sometimes success. I found "letting go some" was one of the most difficult things I would face. Hoping only that my child grew to be successful and valued as a member of society, protecting her was truly my only duty. Allowing her to spend more time away, make crucial decisions, and choose her actions seemed counter to my storybook ending. As we know, children and teens don't always make decisions which are well thought out, considering all aspects and ramifications. Safeguarding our children while allowing them to experience life is tough but necessary to mold them fully.

Although the thought of my children, flying through the air, falling into the waiting arms of their classmates does not rank high on my list of being a grand time, The experience they receive from their hard work and dedication to their sport can set a foundation for success within each of them.

Life Lessons

Understanding that to fully gain the benefit from this awesome thing called life, we must be willing to loosen the reigns we hold over our loved ones, allowing them to experience life and all it safely has to offer. Although difficult, it's imperative. As the week has continued and the girls continue their cheerleading journey, I have become a bit more relaxed. Hearing the girls make good choices and even voice their concern over such a short training season fills the void left by fatherly fear and replaces those fears with excitement over attending their demonstration. Of course, good old dad will be seated on the front row ready to spring into action and catch them if they fall. That's just what we do.

Chapter 34

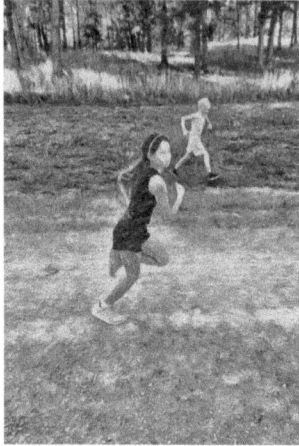

Getting Sidetracked is Easy

My beautiful wife and I began our journey last week with the intention of simply watching both of our girls compete in their second cross country race. Having been forced to miss their first meet due to prior obligations, we were rather excited to take part in the process of cheering on our little ladies. As we followed the school bus to the location of the competition, the natural surroundings and calmness added to our ultimate relaxation and enjoyment of the time away from our busy schedules. The natural beauty of the location which was chosen for the race overshadowed our memories of past meets where the long walk to the start and finish line tested the will of not only the competitors but likewise the parents who chose to attend and cheer on the young athletes striving to find their moment of fame.

As we followed the directions of the parking attendants, my angst began to rise, as I watched the long string of vehicles parked along the roadway. With much regret, well, honestly not too much regret, this past year has not been the best for me fitness wise and with the added cheeseburgers, cake, and other delicious options out there my year has been one of added weight and declined endurance. With my awesome "dad bod" on full display I did my best to convince my mind that it was for the girls, and I would surly make it without the ambulance being called. As we exited, I commented to my wife about the beauty of the area and how excited I was about the race. Her grimace told the tale that she, just like me, was less than enthused about the long walk we were about to embark up on.

To our surprise, as we exited our vehicle and prepared for our journey on foot, we were met with one of the most beautiful things I can recall seeing in quite a while. The pristine golf cart, parked directly behind our vehicle, was intended to shuttle us to the location where viewing the race would be easier, according to the young driver. Surprised, yet grateful, my looked at each other and jointly experienced a sigh of relief. The couple in the vehicle next to us evidently had similar thoughts and feelings because although the cart was nearer to me, I could see the man looking intently. Like the scene from an old western movie the man and I stood several yards apart, sun glistening, breeze slight, we were preparing for the showdown. A showdown where the prize was a one-way trip of luxury along the winding path of the elementary cross-country world. I knew it was now or never, so I quickly motioned to my wife, who evidently saw the duel unfolding and was very committed to secure our escort. Quickly we preserved our seats. I won't lie, I may have inadvertently smiled as I waived at my momentary adversary while we drove away, wishing them the best, as they waited for their ride.

As we arrived at the playing field the mood was electric. With excitement abounding, we wished our little athletes well and passed on little tidbits of strategy to each of them. My wife and I had decided that I would remain at the start line and Leona would hurry to the finish line where I would meet her after both girls made it past my location. As I heard the starting gun, I watched as one of our girls ran by. A short time later our second passed me, smiling, and taking in her newly found adventure. When out of sight, I quickly moved towards the finish line which was a couple hundred yards away. As I arrived, I could see Lilli across the lake nearing the final turn to the finish. I could see she was in a tough battle with another athlete, and I instantaneously became "that parent". My encouraging voice and cheers for my child could be audibly heard across the lake and I'm relatively certain throughout the county. As Lilli crossed the finish line, I felt a pride for her accomplishment and refusal to succumb to the agony of long-distance running. I quickly congratulated her and turned my attention to the far side of the lake where her sister could be seen.

Shouts of encouragement and excitement again flowed from my mouth as Riyann coasted into the finish line, encouraging another little girl she had met along the path of the race. Watching as she turned towards the little girl, we were almost certain that Riy was going to allow the girl to finish before her so the girl would feel good. Finishing the race, Riyann walked up to the girl and provided some encouraging words. Without hesitation, she then walked up to her mother and began showing her the feather she had found along the way. Describing she found the feather while she was running, my wife and I stood in awe at the pure innocence of the child.

Although spending countless hours talking to the girls about the fine art of competitive sports the concept simply hadn't taken hold in Riyann's mind. For her it was more about the journey along the way. Like the flowers she had found while training, she had come across a beautiful feather along the pathway and simply had to grasp it so she could show her mother and me.

Life Lesson

Be willing to get sidetracked sometimes my friends. Life is difficult and centering constantly on the finish, avoiding all the flowers and feathers along the way, results in a pretty bland adventure. For Riy, the pain and suffering of cross-country are made bearable because of the friends she meets, and relationships she builds along the way... that and the awesome and beautiful things she discovers along the way. I so want to grow up to be like this child!

Chapter 35

A Watchful Eye

Working hard to leave a viable legacy to my children has always been important to me. Recently, while working on our newest family venture, a small restaurant attached to our motel, I was talking with my wife as both of my youngest children scurried around, in and out, as children routinely do. As I looked outside the building in an attempt to gain sight of my kids to ensure they were safely playing, my eyes rested upon a sight which caused my heart to jump and mind to envision perfection.

As a young person I became introduced to the art of photography. Over the years the art has grown into a full-blown obsession where I seemingly am constantly in a state of exploration for the perfect photograph. My camera and I have adventured far and wide as my attempts of refining my eyes have become good at times and occasionally great but more than most, mediocre yet rewarding to this man with desire to create.

As I looked out upon our property, attempting to pinpoint the location of my youngest, my eyes fell upon her. Nestled with a nearby bush, seated upon a large rock, my child sat. With seemingly no care or motivation evident, Riyann simply gazed forth into the horizon. As I noticed her pose my mind immediately raced to the thought that I had to capture the moment which undoubtably would result in an award -winning shot. I quickly retained my photographic gear and quietly moved into position. Following getting a multitude of shots my child discovered me and went about her normal routine of fleeing to the playground where she was intent upon showing her good old dad the latest trick she had learned.

Following watching and showering her with compliments I quickly rushed to my desk and downloaded the perfect picture, depicting the solitude of youth. Before me, in all its glory, truly was the perfect photograph, at least in this daddy's eyes. Showing it to others brough silent contemplation, smiles and eventual congratulations over capturing such an impactful scene. I went as far as doing something I had never done before with one of my photographs, I entered into a contest hoping the world would see this awesome photo of a awesome child. To my dismay, no comment or selection was made by the judge so I would be satisfied with my simple enjoyment of the image.

Life Lessons

As I gazed upon the image which now hangs in the business, I find happiness. As I

listen to the comments of guests as they peer upon the canvas I feel joy, not simply because of the accomplishment of capturing such art but of my knowledge of the symbolism. I think about how even as with children, the hustle and bustle of our everyday life can overwhelm us momentarily. Taking a moment to sit in a shaded place and gaze upon the horizon.

Chapter 36

Unconditional Love on Display

I t just felt it was right to expound our normal discussion on family to include a very special group. To some, the thought of spotlighting this chosen group defies logic but to others, to all those willing to truly consider the groups impact on us throughout life, the thought of bringing our feelings to the surface is welcome and, in some cases, overdue. In saying this, the events of the past couple of weeks in my household and our recent loss of one of our beloved pets, Isie, caused me to truly think about the impact the family pet has on our homes and all those who live within it.   Regardless of whether it's a fuzzy little puppy, adventurous kitten, slithering reptile, or feathery fowl, many of us have had our lives impacted by the friendships we build with our pet.

As a young child, the inclusion of the family pet was not abnormal. For our family, the bond between child and pet primarily focused on dogs. Although mom loved cats, her allergies and those of my sister wouldn't allow us to experience the household cat so to my joy, another form of four-legged excitement became the norm. Growing up we had several dogs, all unique in their own special ways. Whether it was the miniature Terrier-Poodle mix, Tiny two, the fuzzy sheepdog, or my prized Golden German Shepard Baron, I found unconditional love and companionship. My furry friends provided a place to lay my head, a shoulder to cry on, and a set of ears to listen to all my problems, all while looking intently and simply said, loving me regardless. They stood between mom and

I when I was about to receive my just reward for misbehaving, taking the brunt of her frustration upon themselves. Looking back, I still chuckle as I rewind that moment in my m ind.

As I grew, becoming a man, Dogs always played a pivotal role throughout my life. Just like when I was a child, the one thing I could always depend upon was their presence. Regardless of the how my day went, whether good or bad it really didn't matter. If I was feeling sick or on top of the world, depressed, or just fine, when I opened the front door, my pet would be waiting for me with a smile and joy in their hearts. For little did I know that I was the center of their life just like they were to me.

Always there to share the joys of promotions, relationships, births and holidays, my pets never once let me down. Sure, there were rough moments, just like we all have with our pet's. But in the end, the matter remained that these furry little creatures truly must be placed in our paths by God to lessen the burdens felt and to provide a snout on the shoulder when times just seemed too much to bear. I've learned that these creatures, considered dumb by most, truly are much more intelligent than most give them credit f or.

I make this assertion simply through experience. Regardless of if it is the puppy who gets excited when it senses you are near, or the cat that decides it's time to rub against you, the timing seems perfect. Picking their humans, our pets may bond more with one family member but readily display love and adoration to all, many times showing a willingness to lay down their own lives to further the life of family members. As I earlier stated my family lost one of our key family members this week. Isie, was a special girl. Choosing her momma as her human she never neglected showing each member of the family love. Although a momma's girl, she wrestled and smiled with the best of them while maintaining her proverbial classiness around her momma. This deep devotion was evident even up to the end.

As her strength drew less, it was apparent that she would only be with us for a time. In my mind, Issie fully understood this and did her best to lessen the impact on momma, her beloved human. This was seen by me on at least two occasions this week. Understanding that her momma was hurting, issie held out, in my opinion, until her momma reluctantly left to carry out some required business before she said her final goodbye. I have no doubt this fragile little girl felt her momma would be better off not seeing it and held out accordingly, trusting daddy to prepare momma and make her look presentable when her mom arrived. Oh, what an awesome, loving, cuddly, little girl she was and is.

I smile a little more because of having them in my life. With each pets passing I find it more and more difficult to find solace. Although the pain seems to compound, I find joy in having experienced time with them. The lessons I have learned about fair play, letting yourself have a little fun, and how to unconditionally treat those around me is simply because of my four-legged friends. Silly as it may seem, they are true heroes to me. The true companionship felt, and emotion experienced cannot be minimized because you truly want nothing more than to see us happy. For our pets, we say thank you, we can never repay your devotion. Hold them a little tighter tonight, my friends, for we never know when they will merely be a series of lessons, experiences, and memories, designed to fill our hearts full of love, always reminding us of what it truly means to give of yourself.

Life Lesson

The lessons we learn from the addition of pets into our lives are boundless. Their unconditional love and commitment to each of us is an inspiration for bettering ourselves.

Chapter 37

Along for the Ride

As I walked out to my truck, I could hear the scampering of little feet behind me. I turned to look and watched as my child scurried to the passenger side of the vehicle and began climbing in. Once securely inside I asked my daughter what she was doing. Without hesitation, and never looking up, she secured her seat belt and said, "coming with ya dad". I explained that I was wasn't going anywhere in particular and my journey would not be exciting so if she preferred to hang out at home, she was welcome to. As she looked up, I could see her beautiful bright eyes glimmering in the light as she began responding to my offer. With a coy smile affixed to her face, she simply said "it's ok daddy, I just like being with you".

As we traveled down the road with no particular destination in mind, we laughed, we joked, and we sat in silence, taking in the beauty of the area and each other's company. As a breeze of contentment flowed over me, I couldn't fight back the emotion of happiness for being so overly blessed in this life. The entire scene was reminiscent of many years prior when as a young father I was asked to coach my local high school varsity basketball team. At that time working full-time, engaged in extra duties within the departments specialized teams, and raising my eldest daughter seemed to fill my days and nights. Being faced with the opportunity of coaching, I couldn't refuse. The position added to my busy schedule but created within itself an avenue of enjoyment and accomplishment.

I remember all the late nights and weekends spent practicing, attending camps, and traveling to games. At the time, time seemed to be passing by faster than my team could make it down the court. Being young, I failed to recognize that adding things to my schedule many times took away from other aspects of life. Before long, my daughter began "tagging along" as the team did what teams do. Refusing to let dad go at his newly found job alone, she explained that I always needed to know that someone in the family supported me and her being there was proof. I remember looking down as my daughter lay sleeping, while the team bus traveled down the road, returning from a tough loss. It was then that the entire concept of commitment became cemented in my mind and soul.

Life Lessons

Life carries with it many opportunities. Opportunities to serve, expand and move forward accomplishing great things along the way. We can excel and become the richest, most proficient person in town, never leaving any stone unturned but if we forget the true value of commitment we are lost. For it is in the silent smiles, gentle touch, and simply being with those we love and care for that we will find true solace. Find that person you simply want to be around and revel in the enjoyment of each other my friends. This is where you will find fulfillment and true contentment.

Chapter 38

The Tears of the Innocent

Those who are familiar with my little family, understand that my youngest daughter, Riyann, is an adventurous child who for the most part cares minimally about fitting in but rather draws contentment from her keen sense of artistic fervor and exploration. This being said, I do not think I've ever met such a kind and compassionate person throughout my travels. She will joyfully hand you a shirt when your chilled, a hug when you are down and is always ready to provide the best possible shoulder massage those little eight-year-old hands can give when she senses you are stressed. She cares not about material things and is routinely the recipient of her mother and my lectures about the importance of saving her money due to her truly caring nothing about it. She would rather find joy giving her hard-earned dollars to someone she senses is in need than worrying about placing it in her piggy bank or purse.

Riyann has never been a child who looks forward to school and the contained learning which is associated therein. This year, to our glee, she routinely comes home from a long day at school with a smile on her face, bearing stories of fun and friendship as she discloses the particulars about her day making sure we know that although her teacher makes them do entirely too much arithmetic, she is still the best teacher ever. This past week Riyann, during one of her adventures, came across a skinny yellow cat which had undoubtedly been dropped off at the motel.

Riyann and the cat began the bonding process as she conveniently experienced a total loss of hearing when it came to her mother and my repeated direction not to bother the animal. As the days passed by us, I would routinely see Riyann showing the cat affection as she played with the feline, she named Mittens. Although feral, Mittins appeared to sense that this child's true intent and showed no aggressive behavior. The animal soon realized that my child would play with it while making it the center of this child's universe and would routinely tag along wherever the child went.

Upon closing one evening I returned to the main office in the dark of the evening. As I approached the door a small glimmer of light caught my eye. As I turned to look, I observed Riyann, seated in a chair watching her iPad while stroking the cat as it lay on an adjacent chair with its head gently resting upon the leg of the child. This became indicative of the next several days. We would return home; Riyann would exit our vehicle to the welcoming meows of her newest friend. Our attempts to warn the child about the dangers the animal faced outside and her need to not become too attached fell on deaf ears. For her desire to care for her new friend superseded any thought of the animal one day not being there to welcome her home.

Yesterday, that unfortunate day came. Although necessary and in the best interest of little mittens, a caring guest likewise fell in love with the truly loving animal. Speaking her desire to adopt Mittens and provide her with a stable home and our being unable to provide the same for the animal due to medical reasons within the family we graciously agreed, and Mittens began his new journey. As a side note, the guest has graciously kept us updated on the travels of Mittens and how he has adjusted well to his new surroundings.

Wondering how I would explain this to Riyann and hoping she would understand began overshadowing my thoughts. As the day passed by the thought left my mind. As I continued with my daily routine I came to the point where I went to pick my daughters up from school. As I sat in the parking lot, watching RIyann play with her friends I noted that she seemed to be having a good day. Her smile was energizing as she spun on the playground equipment. Upon her entry into the vehicle she, with excitement, described how her class did well and as a reward didn't have to take a test the following day but rather got to watch a movie. Her joy brought a little skip in my heart.

As we approached our destination, I explained the normal post school regiment we would need to complete and watched as Riyann quickly opened her door. As I did the same, I observed Riyann ducking around looking in the bushes and under cars all the while calling out for her friend Mittens. At that moment my heart sank as I contemplated how to best explain the situation surrounding her friend. As I pulled her aside and began explaining she immediately dropped to her knees and the emotion flowed forth. Unfortunately, no amount of consoling would mend this broken heart.

Explaining to me that Mittens was her friend and the only friend she could sit with and talk to when she was having a "real bad day" elephant tears flowed forth. We sat for a time as I attempted to explain, and she countered my every word with tears and the logic of an eight -year- old we made it through. The evening consisted of many tears, hugs, and printing pictures of her and her little Mittens. Plans were devised to print her a t-shirt with a picture of she and Mittens on it and a portrait placed on her wall as the child began recovering from her loss. As my head hit my pillow on this night the thoughts of being a young man losing my best friend, Barron due to disease flooded my mind, giving me a greater understanding of what Riyann was going through.

Today, although not forgotten, Mittens is no longer the cause of great sorrow. As we traveled to school we talked and joked as Lilli, Riyann's sister did her best to understand what her younger sister was going through. Choosing the song, we would listen to traveling to school Riyann chose the cat song, which in all reality consisted of nothing but "meows" giving their rendition of a popular pop classic as she and I laughed while her sister didn't enjoy it as much, sitting, arms crossed in bewilderment over how quickly her sister and dad had lost their minds.

Life Lessons

Life is riddled with pain, hurt, and disappointment. Although a natural byproduct of our existence we must remind ourselves that showing humanity and compassion to others as they travel through the pain of loss is essential. To Riyann, her loss was devastating, and her world was seemingly coming to an end; just as mine was over forty years ago when my best friend Barron went to the vet to never return. Understanding that life goes on and we must cherish the moments we have is difficult, almost as difficult as seeing someone we love dearly experience pain. At times words are not sufficient and all we can do is reach out and provide a warm, caring shoulder. For it is through us that our younger generations will find direction, coping, and true compassion.

Chapter 39

Believing adds Confidence

A s I listened to the girls provide me with a rundown of their day, I was amazed at the progress one of my daughters has been making with her schoolwork. For her, school has always been difficult. Driven by nature and the world around her, the thought of sitting idle in a classroom, falling victim to a barrage of meaningful facts being thrown at her was pointless and to be quite simply a waste of her time. This behavioral attribute alongside a rather severe learning disability, created barriers which the child simply couldn't overcome. Having all this in mind we decided to mix things up a bit this year. Being committed to the success of our children my wife and I decided to remove the girls from the traditional learning environment and embark upon the home school journey.

Following conducting exhaustive research into which curriculum would not only meet our children's needs, educationally, and provide flexibility with true learning we chose a program and excitedly set the day of starting. After a short time, it was evident that our children were thriving and to be truthful, receiving a more advanced education than they had received prior. Now don't get me wrong, this in no way is meant to reflect poorly on our current educational system, but rather, show our journey of discovery. Throughout the girl's prior education in the public school system, we have been blessed with, in my opinion, some of the best teachers around. What we found was that with our children it was a time issue.

Our child's ability to receive the time necessary for her to fully grasp the necessary concepts were simply impossible until we ventured out on our own. Monitoring full classrooms while doing their best to spark lights withing each child became an over-whelming task for educators when recognizing that some students struggle. Taking the necessary time with each student to ensure they were thriving became an insurmountable task, leaving those struggling to simply be moved to a realm of lower expectations. This is what made our choice more viable.

Early on my wife discovered that time bread confidence and that confidence in turn created expectations within our child. The more encouragement and one on one time we were able to provide, the fuller the child's learning would evolve and exceed expectations. Stunned by the rapid turn of events, I watched on as my wife planted the belief deep with-in a child that she to was intelligent and could learn. This simple belief then blossomed in a desire to learn and excel, even beating her sister on scoring, the same sister she has looked up to for her entire life as being the most intelligent one around.

As I sit, proud of both my children and their mother who works so hard at their education I joyfully am the recipient of lengthy descriptions from my child about the solar system and the earth's core. Although, schoolwork is the last thing on my mind many days and hearing lengthy recaps of the days newly discovered concepts, rarely seems like fun to me, I will take it in stride, because it comes from my child and her excitement to learn.

Life Lesson

As we venture forward my friends, never lose sight of the fact that the simple act of believing in someone can many times change lives. Putting aside all the thoughts that something can't be done and centering on how we can make it happen. Belief and showing a willingness to step outside the proverbial box and find innovative approaches to challenges fosters true learning and confidence which can and most assuredly will change lives and our world for the better. Welcome innovation my friends and never stop seeing what could be if we simply believe.

Chapter 40

Bringing Smiles

T he long-awaited gift arrived. My anticipation was high and as I opened the box. My excitement could barely be contained. Just like a child opening the door to a brightly lit candy store for the first time, I took on the role of child as my wife looked on with a bewildered look on her face. Undoubtedly, her mind was thinking about how it was time to ground me from Amazon, again, but she quietly looked on, shaking her head. To help you understand, and to set the framework for understanding about this box, I'll explain. Last year was the first year I decided that I would join in with the girls and take part in dressing up in a costume for Halloween. Choosing the best family costume, my wife grudgingly went along as we planned and prepped for the big festival where we would showcase our transformation. When it was all said and done, we had a lot of fun and I won the best costume trophy, which did nothing more than fueled my desire to make the outing an annual occurrence, to the rest of the family's dismay.

Deciding upon this year's costume choice was a no brainer although the rest of the family refused to buy in. Luckily, we have plenty of time for me to convince them that father knows best. Learning that buying costumes brings fun with the girls to an entirely new level I have repeatedly been advised that buying the latest latex mask, outfit, and fabricated fur suite was simply a waste of hard-earned dollars. This box was nothing more than an extension of adventures, smiles, and fun its contents would surely provide. As I opened the box which contained the latest in my long line of fun seeking props the gears of my mind began turning about when the best time to implement it would be.

Over the past two years a joke has grown between Lilli, my ten- year- old and I. With the completion of every movie which contains a forest scene, drive down a road which is wooded, or generally any outdoor type outing, I repeatedly tell her she needs to be on the lookout for Big Foot. Describing that Big Foot is a quiet creature who doesn't like to be seen, Lilli routinely counters my descriptions with a look of disgust, voicing her disbelief in the creature. Lilli's skepticism is brought to the surface as she described that I know better and it's hard to see a thing which doesn't exist. Although convincing, good ol dad, in the traditional dad way, simply disregards her skepticism and carries on with the tradition of vigilance.

Smiling as I began unboxing my recent purchase, I was convinced that I would prove my ten-year-old wrong and have a little fun along the way. My wife, still shrugging her head in disbelief over the fact that this intelligent adult could find such joy over a silly, pointless purchase, smiled and I'm sure considered if it was time to put me out to pasture. As I removed the perfectly designed big foot costume my excitement grew. I explained, again how we would play the perfect practical joke on our child, which without a doubt would resonate throughout history as the best dad prank ever.

The day of the great reveal finally came and as our family settled down for a quiet evening at home, I found it impossible to wait any longer. As the thunder sounded outside the house, my wife explained it would be best for us to wait because it appeared the rain would start at any moment. Refusing to take no for an answer, I reiterated the game plan and retired to the basement to prepare. As I dawned the bulky, fur bearing suit, my youngest giggled at the lengths dad was taking to have some fun. Like an angelic choir, I heard my cell phone ring, notifying me that the girls were in position. My co-conspirator wife, would take Riyann onto the back deck of the house where they would look at the sunset. As with any pre-teen, Lillie would be curious over what her mom and sister were doing and follow. As the trio, stood on the deck, talking about God's great gift of nature, I would make my way up from the basement.

I will admit, I was a bit uneasy as I exited the house and began walking through the driveway to the side yard where I would make my grand entrance. Luckily for me, no trucks full of road hunters came by. As I made my way, quietly through the trees I could hear the girls talking about nature. Once positioned perfectly I began shaking tree branches then quickly walked into an open space between the tree line and house where the talk turned to silence and gasps. As planned, I briskly walked along the tree line, looking up towards the girls, grunting occasionally. The gasps and silence quickly turned to laughter as Lilli began talking about what she had just observed.

Life Lesson

Although refusing to give in and admit that good old dad fooled her, Lilli, Riy and momma laughed and experienced a moment of fun at the hands of their dad who was nearing a heat stroke. I think about how taking the time to lose yourself in the fun, refusing to remain so stringent and proper while simply having fun playing together can many times mean everything in a family. With each passing day there seems to be unsurmountable stress and worry over our world and the safety of the family unit. Take the time to goof around a little bit with your loved ones my friends. For it is when we bring smiles to the ones, we love that fighting through the process becomes bearable.

Chapter 41

Bumps and Bruises

With the emergence of the sun, finally showing through the cloudy sky, our little family has been feverishly preparing our business for the summer tourist season. Although the girls have struggled to wrap their minds around the importance of hard work, specifically not having the opportunity to sleep in on the weekends, they have truly rose to the task of working hard to accomplish our goals. Riyann, taking the early morning wake ups hard, has ensured that we all understand her distain for early mornings and little down time she has been able to enjoy. Trying to convince her that she gets to sleep in an additional two hours on non-school days is pointless because to this child sleeping in entails waking up a little after lunch time.

Last week I continued working on the new building while I allowed the girls to tag along and pretty much hang out and play while occasionally grabbing a hammer or pain brush to assist. The day was going great. I worked, while having the opportunity to listen to the joyful ramblings of my children outside the door as they played, giggled, and competed. Realistically, a joyful noise was not exactly what I was hearing. Anyone with young children fully understands that although possessing a deep love for their siblings, children tend to spend very little time "joyfully conversing" rather, the time is filled with arguing, fighting, and multi-faceted discourse. Although laughing at some overheard comments, my day was truly filled with wondering when I may have to intercede to ensure the continued existence of my offspring.

Without notice, my youngest burst through the single, old style, glass door. Franticly, she described that she was minding her own business, talking to a rather large bumble bee when out of nowhere, her elder sister rushed up, striking the bee with her foot, sending it to the happy pollinating lands in the sky. In a state of disbelief, Riyann told me she just couldn't believe her sister killed the bee. Looking towards Lilli, she simply shrugged her shoulders and looked off with the apparent purpose to communicate, "yeah.... I did it.... Oh well". Finding it in-consequential, I simply described to Riyann that I was sure her sister was merely attempting to protect her.

Not accepting my response, Riyann insisted that I go along with her so I could see the corpse of the bumble bee. Reluctantly, I agreed and as I exited the doorway, Riyann ensured that she told me the story a third time. As I turned to empathize with the child, I began seeing the very scene which as a parent we fear. Watching, in slow motion, our child get hurt while not having an ability to intercede quick enough is hard on a dad. As I looked, I saw the door close with Riy's hand in the frame pinning her fingers. Quickly I pushed the door and dislodged her hand. As She cried in pain, I had not option other than doing what I do best, I held her tight and attempted to ease her suffering.

As we dealt with the pain of a pinched finger, Riyann, angrily shouted a series of words which to be honest, made it difficult not to laugh. "What's up with Karma?" "It was Lilli that killed the bee", She yelled. She went on to described that she simply didn't understand. She revealed that she was the kind one and yet she was the one who always got hurt... "it just isn't right". As we comforted her, and she began feeling better we decided that our work was done for the day, and it would be best to head home.

Life Lesson

While driving, I thought about the fact that no matter how hard we work in life, sometimes bad things happen, leaving us with confusion about what we could have done differently to avoid heartache. It just doesn't seem fair. Hard work includes bumps and bruises but one thing I know for sure is that through those hurts, we find that our pain many times fosters success and wisdom in the face of adversity. Don't be afraid to work hard at achieving our goals my friends, keeping everything in its right perspective. Put aside the bumps and bruises and simply enjoy talking to the bees.

Chapter 42

Comfort Doesn't Outweigh Commitment

B eing the single parent of a bright ten -year- old daughter brought new challenges and adventures, sometimes on a daily basis. Life it seemed had transitioned from that of ease to one of scheduling, no sleep, and fear. With no end in sight, I simply held on and did the best I could as a young father. I recall when my eldest daughter was finishing up elementary school it was important to me, that my child knew I was fully committed to her regardless of the challenges. Little did I know or in all reality understand the depths which this thing called parenthood would take me.

One aspect I truly enjoyed about parenting is the opportunity to tag along as the kids get to go on adventures such as field trips and classroom parties. I recall the excitement I felt, when given the opportunity to partake and travel alongside the other parents as we relived our youth through our children as they explored and spread their adventurous wings. As a parent, I had the opportunity to spend time with my child as they embarked upon educational fun. What could be better.

I recall Natalie being overly excited one year to take part in the annual end of the school year field day. As we prepared for the event, she could barely contain her excitement as she spoke of trying hard and winning as many event ribbons as she could. Encouraging her to give it her best I recall the feelings of competition overtaking me as I graced her with the latest strategies and tactics designed to ensure her success. As I drove to the designated field and waited for the arrival of the student's I thought about what a beautiful day it had turned out to be along the front range of Colorado. I watched as several other parents arrived. Hoping to secure the best location possible and of course show how awesome of a dad I was I assembled alongside the sparsely positioned parents.

Engaging in small talk, I was doing pretty well holding my own with the other ultra-competitive parents. As we spoke about a wide variety of things, I fit right in despite my lengthy six-foot seven frame and newly laundered dad shorts which I had spent hours picking out. I've learned over the years what we as parents wear is just as important as what we say. To embarrass our offspring within their peer group although fun at times, heck even necessary every now and then, results in nothing more than disaster. It was then that a factor I hadn't considered was brought to my attention. While hanging out, looking cool, and playing the part, a petit young mother looked around, then up at me. Unaware if she peered in pure enlightenment over my awesome dad bod adorned in my new knee length surfer shorts or if it was something else, surely it was something else, she hesitated then looked away.

Being intrigued, I continued watching on as the school buses arrived. Without hesitation, and without remorse, this mother moved closer, looked up and whispered the words which would cause my feelings of excitement to rapidly deplete and be replaced with those of unease and self-consciousness. Although simplistic and surely with the best of intentions this mother simply said to me "wow, do you realize you're the only dad that ever comes to these things?"

Immediately, my thoughts flowed to this polite, little lady getting inside my head. Although not a bad thing, the idea of me being the only male in a sea of feminine competitive forces left an uneasy air about the place. Finding myself questioning if the other mothers would react the same or even provide the same advice to their children became my plight for the day. For the remainder of the event, I did my best to put on the best face possible as my child engaged her competitive side. Realizing that lone mother was right, with each turn and each glance where my eyes only found moms. I too was a mom that day, and the days and events that followed. For being a sing parent caused us to take on both roles. Although being the only male there, they welcomed me into the fold and treated me like one of their own.

Thinking back, that day began with excitements and plans for adventure throughout. Through the words of one person, my day shifted to unease and an awareness that I was different then everyone else, not better, or worse, simply different. This is where my true adventure would unfold, and I would learn a lesson about life itself.

Life Lessons

Friends, throughout life we are faced with situations where we are committed to doing things in a manner which brings us success. Every now and then, things happen where our comfort level, while accomplishing that commitment is challenged. It is up to each of us to ensure that as our comfort level subsidies our commitment remains unchanged. Commitment does not require comfort, merely perseverance. I continued attending events, being the only dad, wearing those awful shorts, and enjoying the bond my attendance fostered with my child. Besides, being a part of the "mom group" taught me the true value of parental commitment and competitive friendship along with many tricks, which would help me with my daughter, along the way.

Chapter 43

Committed to Excellence

O ne of the benefits of adulthood is we can envision goals and then act appropriately toward meeting our goals. Seemingly, it all boils down to our choice of acting or not. I recall several years ago attending a conference for my job. While planning, my wife and I decided that it would be the perfect time to pack up the family and make a mini vacation out of the trip, so the girls and Leona came along. Following my conference responsibilities, we suited the girls up and enjoyed some relaxation while the little ones ventured into the swimming pool at the hotel. While watching the girls play and learn to swim my wife and I discussed the benefits of having a swimming pool at our home. Long story short, the universe aligned and rather than constructing a pool at the house we were blessed to purchase a small family motel, yes, even equipped with a swimming pool.

As summer bore down upon us the girls spent many of their afternoons and evenings in the pool, splashing around, doing their best to become proficient in the art of swimming. It was apparent that during these swimming adventures our eldest daughter, Lilli, was determined to show her little sister the ropes as well as ensuring that all rules and safety protocols were strictly adhered to. It was during one of these adventures that Lilli experienced the first dent in her "older sister" armor.

Anyone that has had the pleasure of meeting Lilli understands that she is an extremely driven child. Her desire to help others, including her sister, has at times become overwhelming for the young child but she refuses to give up and consistently attempts to exert her elder knowledge and abilities. With only fourteen months separating her from her sister Riyann, Lilli is truly committed to be a mentor to the younger sibling even in the times of routine sisterly battling. One aspect of youth which Lilli has struggled with is understanding that even though she is older than her sister, there are times Riyann will exceed her. Whether it was losing a tooth first, or running faster, or coloring a better picture Lilli simply cannot accept if her sister achieves something before, she does.

Lilli's extremely competitive nature was brought to the forefront a couple years ago as the girls mother worked with both of them as they learned the art of diving into the pool. Not wanting to interject, I decided to sit along the pool side and watch as the trio interacted and the girls, filled with giggling and laughter, did their best to dive into the swimming pool, head first. After very little prompting, Riyann performed the perfect forward dive into the pool. Following a great deal of excitement and congratulatory words, Riyann beamed with pride as she continued to dive in the pool repeatedly, even giving her sister advice on diving, which didn't go over well as you could imagine. Lilli on the other hand was having no part of it. The look of pure disdain filled her face as she tried and tried again to dive as her mother instructed. Being unsuccessful, Lilli's frustration increased with each perfect dive performed by her sister until the time she simply stated she was tired and was going to get out of the pool. Understanding the true reason for her departure we tried to encourage her to not give up, but she had, had enough for the day.

Later that evening our family gathered in the living room preparing to watch a movie. As we engaged in small talk, I noticed Lilli was nowhere to be found. I walked upstairs where I found Lilli seated on her bed watching her iPad. I inquired as to what she was doing when she replied she was just studying. As we spoke, I learned that Lilli, upon returning from the pool, immediately began watching videos on her iPad which showed the process of diving into a swimming pool. Smiling, I had no choice but to allow her to continue along her journey of recovering her pride through a resurgence of her dominance over her little sister by not only learning to dive but by diving better. Lilli continued studying video's the entire evening, refusing to admit defeat.

Lilli's commitment to exceed her sisters' abilities, although cute on the surface, has become a rallying point for the elder sibling. As with this instance, Lilli has learned that if she struggles with something she need only put her time in to find success. Her commitment to research, study, and practice has thus far allowed her to not only ultimately conquer her defeats but likewise excel in life. As I think about my child, I am reminded about just how often we stumble throughout life. Maybe it's at work, accomplishing tasks, or at home. Failure is at times unavoidable but if we are committed to success, if we put in our time to study and learn from our mistakes, we will surely succeed and before long be diving into the deep end. Lilli successfully learned to dive the next day and again began enjoying her time at the pool. Rather than succumbing to her inability, she overcame and showed that a commitment to excellence will in the end overshadow any failure.

Life Lessons

We can all learn a lesson from Lilli's perseverance, for it is through hard work, preparation, and commitment that excellence is realized.

Chapter 44

Content With Where We Are

Seated, I noticed my daughter looking at my wallet, which I had placed on the center console of my vehicle. As I watched, she described that she thinks she is going to take a look at my wallet to see what dads keep in there. Being a bit amused, I agreed, awaiting her inquiry as to why dads are relatively boring and don't keep necessary items such as hygiene, hair, and always make up by their trusty side. As she looked through each compartment, she spoke when she got to the important part, the money folds. "let's just see how much money you have in here" she said, with a somewhat skeptical tone. A grin filled my face, knowing that I had spent my last paper money a few days earlier when I found the perfect dresser for our suites and hadn't felt the need to replace it as of that point.

With a downtrodden look on her face, the child looked up and simply said "daddy, you don't have any money". I explained that she didn't need to worry because I had plenty money available if needed through my debit card. She seemed to take my reply halfheartedly as she drew silent. What happened next both caused me to pause as well as feel great pride in this little human I have been blessed to have in my life. I watched as the child quickly opened her purse and dug out a twenty-dollar bill and a ten-dollar bill. Anticipating that she was preparing to place her hard-earned money inside my wallet, I assured her that I was not hurting for money and that she did not need to give me her money. Following a short debate, the child simply said OK and played like she was focusing on something different. Continuing to observe the child, I watched as she secretly placed the two bills inside my wallet, closed it, and placed it back on the console.

A couple days later I watched as my child re-checked my wallet and was amazed that the two, crisp bills were still present. Asking me why I hadn't spent the money she gave me, I replied that I was holding it for her. She corrected me abruptly, advising me that she did not need the money and wanted me to have it. A couple days later I approached my daughter, asking her if she was interested in a new job I found around the motel. Saying that she was interested I explained that if she would water the new shrubs and fruit trees we had planted, daily, I would give her five dollars per week. She gladly accepted the offer but explained that she felt she should do it for one dollar because five dollars was simply too much, and she really didn't need any money. The negotiation continued as I agreed, and she accepted, that her pay rate would be one dollar per day for the chore.

As I thought about the two examples of my child and money as well as my wife and I's repeated attempts to teach her the value of money, I considered not only how we have dreadfully failed in our attempts thus far to teach her the importance of financial management, but also how truly special this child is. Being content with where she is in life and what she has, the child thinks first about meeting the needs of others rather than herself. She has found joy in helping others which in the end has made our attempts a success of sorts. Although it is difficult not to force her to strict guidelines which we know will benefit her, understanding and our commitment against stifling the child's spirit has allowed her the experience of receiving a blessing for blessing others.

For it is when we can be content in our present situation and the place in life that we reside that our ability to truly give from the heart to meet the needs of others can be emboldened. Giving is not always found in the form of monetary items or possessions but many times in a simple act of kindness.

Life Lessons

Be content my friends, worry little about what we can get out of life but rather center on what each of us can add to the lives of those around us. I will continue teaching my daughters about financial management but now, I will do my best to understand what I already know, that relinquishing that piece of paper can at times bring forth greater dividends.

Chapter 45

Dark Days Without the Internet

As we welcomed the hot days of August, our family experienced a humorous yet self-described day of devastation for the girls. Striving to integrate education into our everyday lives Leona, my wife, decided to take the girls along with her as she prepared for the upcoming election. While including the girls, Leona would have a prime opportunity to explain the benefits of the electoral systems in America while ensuring a captive audience from the girls. The day began with excitement and many questions from the girls but rapidly turned to one of boredom and distain, the type which all parents, of younger children who believe they are older than they are, are familiar with.

As the trio completed their duties, they decided to take the rest of the day and do some relaxing at home, playing with the pets and generally doing what families do. A couple hours later, when good old dad made it home it was apparent that something went terribly wrong. While momma showered and prepared for an early bedtime, Riyann, our youngest tucked herself away in her bedroom, playing with her toys as she envisioned the latest adventure she and her dolls were embarking upon. As I found my place on my couch, turned on the television and began surfing the channels, hoping to find something of interest on the channel guide, I noticed a nervous Lilli pacing back and forth in the Livingroom.

Finding Lilli's actions much more interesting than what I was finding on the television I began giving her my full attention. I watched as she moved from one side of the room to the other, exhaling loudly, shoulders limp, explaining that she just didn't know if she was going to make it. Confident that she would surely voice her dismay soon, I simply watched and did my best not to engage the child. As any smart father knows, there are times to engage and others when its best not to poke the adolescent bear when you don't have to. As I watch, Lilli became more and more visual with her body movements and verbal frustration.

She began explaining to me that she was so bored and her little sister wouldn't go outside with her to play. She added that she simply had nothing to do and was uncertain if she would survive the night. As we spoke she explained to me that if she could only use my cell phone for a little bit she thought she may be alright. After explaining that my phone was on the charger, so her using it was out of the question, she again sighed loudly, and I'm pretty sure developed a series of ticks surrounding her eyes and a noticeable shaking of her hands. It was then that it hit me, the internet was out at the house and the child was going through withdrawals from her cherished iPad.

Explaining that she only needed it for a minute, the child was not going to take no for an answer. She pleaded, reasoned, and even stooped to level of bribery at one point, assuring me that those dishes in the sink would miraculously disappear into the realm of cleanliness if I only succumbed and allowed her five minutes of joy, with either my iPad or cell phone. No amount of reasoning was resonating with the child as she felt the full force of her electronics addiction swarm around her. Finding it somewhat humorous, but trying to be empathetic, I described several other items she could be doing even resorting to reverse phycology and explaining that I knew of a child's bedroom which needed cleaned. Simply said, she was having none of it and continued on until she disappeared downstairs, I'd imagine taking part in Riyann's adventure with her babies.

As I contemplated the events of my beloved child's plight, I wondered how we as a people have come so far in such a short time, having the world at our fingertips because of these minicomputers we call phones and tablets. As I considered the positive impacts such devises have on us, I was also confronted with exactly how the devices can possess potential negative effects for each of us. The topic has been a hotbed issue in our family as we have observed an upward surge un usage now that school is out, leaving the girls with a motivation similar to a sleeping sloth absent their devices.

Considering all the good thing's technology can be attributed to in our lives we must be on guard not to lose sight of the vastly important traditional learning curves which many of us grew to despise as children but truly molded our very being. Playing outside, exploring, catching crawdads from the creek and generally being a kid never included a handheld device for many of us. Some may consider it a tragedy, others a blessing. Either way, we learned to look, work, and play outside the box, finding adventure in the simpler things in life. Take the time my friends, the time necessary to put the devices down, encourage the same from our children, and soak in all this world has to offer. Learning to engage our surroundings as we embark upon an adventure of a lifetime. Maybe then, only then, can the pain of device withdrawal be minimized despite all the humor we find therein.

Life Lesson

Put down the devices and experience life every now and then. It is then that true knowledge can flow.

Chapter 46

Don't Stress the Small Stuff

With the present school year entering its final quarter, the girls have begun some of the more enjoyable aspects of elementary school. As a parent we have become accustomed to receiving notifications from teachers about the themes the next week would encompass and then take it upon ourselves to dress the children in a manner consistent with the theme. Longing for the days of old when we as students attended school, daily, in our normal clothing has become pointless with the incursion of motivational education. In saying this, Sunday we were notified that this week would center upon reading, with each day bringing forth an opportunity for the girls to get into character and dress in a manner consistent with a daily theme. Today was a day set aside to celebrate travel and concentrate upon how reading can take you to faraway places, full of excitement and joy.

This travel theme had become a day of interest with the girls. As Lilli spoke, non-stop, about creating a passport and wearing tourist related clothing, Riyann simply sat back and began thinking. Following a brief brainstorming session Riyann inquired as to the possibility of swinging by the motel before we went to school so she could retrieve a dress. Thinking nothing of it, and with my best fatherly thinking, I instantly found an opportunity to make this a win-win situation for everyone involved. You see, each new morning involves a great deal of prodding and wake up reminders for Riyann. She would not be considered a morning person so the struggle getting her up, dressed, and groomed is real. Negotiating the retrieval of the desired dress gave me an opportunity to provide her with some added motivation to get up and start moving rather than seating herself in front of the heater, mediating, or whatever you call her morning routine. I must say I was proud of myself for coming up with the plan and I can attest that it worked perfectly, at least I thought it had.

As I woke my children up, I made sure I reminded Riyann about the fact that she would need to hurry herself if she wished to get her dress. With exact precision, the likes I've never seen before, the child quickly got dressed and readied herself for the adventure of the day before her. While we drove to the motel, her sister revealed that she too needed to retrieve a shirt and following a bit of reminding on my part I dropped the girls off at the door and asked them to hurry as I entered the office to retrieve an item I needed. As I completed my task, I saw a quick flash out of the corner of my eye. The flash was Riyann quickly running to the vehicle and entering back in her place. I thought to myself about just how awesome I must be to be able to finally find a means by which to motivate my babies to recognize and honor time commitments.

Being the last to re-enter the vehicle I asked the girls if they got everything they needed and once I heard the words that they had we started towards the school. Following our normal daily routine, I loved on the girls and spoke of how exciting the day would be and while wishing them well I watched as they excited the vehicle and walked towards their teachers. It was then that my self-prescribed thoughts of awesomeness and being a strategical genius came to a screeching halt and was overtaken by a voice in my head saying, "what on earth is that child wearing". Or better yet, "What on earth is that child wearing.... wait that's my child". In my haste to meet time restraints, and my gloating at my awesome motivational prowess, I had forgotten one of the most important aspects of raising children. That being, given the opportunity, a child will devise the most interesting clothing selection possible if left unrestrained. Their choice can at times leave all viewing their selection in a mode of shock and awe like seen during the commencement of a great military battle.

As I watched my lovely little lady walk away, long dress flowing, looking like a combination of both a goth styled Cindy Lauper and possibly younger version of Stevie Nicks, I noticed a smile on the face of her principal. I'm sure she was attempting to hold back the laughter which was inwardly seeking to burst forth with the primary theme in her head of who would dress their child in this manner. All I could think about was, that will teach you educators to make every day a theme day. Confused still, at what my child was wearing and about how she so elegantly got away with changing, reentry into the vehicle and quietly remaining unnoticed, I began feeling my anxiety rise. It was then that I heard my child reveal to her principal her motivation behind her dress.

The child happily disclosed to her principal that today was a day about how books can help us travel and her outfit symbolized that. The educator then smiled and encouraged the child.

Life Lessons

As I drove away, a calm came over me. I began thinking about how sometimes it's just not worth it to stress the small things in life. For it is when we can be ourselves regardless of what everyone else thinks, it is then that we can fully blossom. Now I'm not advocating allowing our children to choose their clothing consistently, for if we do that there's no telling what this world will come to, but rather not be to be constrained by the confines of societal norms. Maybe that's just what our world needs, more pure hearts willing to explore, finding joy in an old Halloween costume perfect for that day's theme. I'm relatively certain that I will have a lot of explaining to do when my wife sees her chosen clothing for the day, hopefully she too will see the comedy in it all.

Chapter 47

Finding Enjoyment from the Process

Lilli had experienced a disappointing result from her last cross-country race of the year. Competing in the final race of the season yesterday, she rebounded. Following a weeklong series of modifications, strategizing, and telling herself she would do better, she did in fact perform awesome and brought home a medal. As I stood, watching the final race it began as many before had. Lillie excelled and remained in the lead pack of runners the entire race while her sister, Riy was content to do her best, soaking in her surroundings and making new friends towards the rear of the pack.

For anyone who knows Riyann, her best effort includes a great deal of conversation and all-encompassing smiles as she forges her way along the cross-country world. Not quite as advanced as her sister, within the sport, Riyann takes in all the advice you throw at her and seems to forget it all once the starting bell sounds. As I watched my youngest yesterday, struggling to keep up with the other athletes it became apparent to me that this beautiful child simply cared little about the outcome but rather centered upon the experience.

Understanding that not all kids are excited about, committed, nor able to perform within the harsh world of cross country running; my wife and I have praised Riyann about her commitment and genuinely giving the sport a shot. At the same time, we have explained that the sport isn't for everyone and if she chooses not to take part, we were fine with her choice because we were proud of her for giving it her all and following through with her commitment to her school, coaches, and community. Each time we bring the subject of her continuing within the sport, Riyann assures us that she likes being a part of the team and wants to continue.

Watching her struggle forward at last night's race my heart fell for the little girl who found it difficult to find a breath in her tired little body. As she rounded the final corner, finish line in sight, the only words I could summons were "you're doing great, time to kick it in and pass the girl in front of you". Looking as if she fully understood but hadn't decided if it was worth the effort or not, she summonsed the last ounce of energy in her body and finished the race. Upon catching her breath, I watched as this tired little girl transitioned from student athlete to cheerleader as she quickly made her rounds congratulating the other students then ultimately finding a place near the finish line so she could do her best to encourage the boys who had begun their race.

As I watched my child, loudly cheer on the little guys, regardless of their affiliation, her words of "come on, you can do it" sounded throughout the valley and to be quite honest, summoned a great deal of pride within me. For Riy, I realize, winning the race was a great idea and being lucky enough to win a medal would be awesome but more important than either of those was simply being there. She thrived on being a part of the team and running along as parents, grandparents, friends, and foes cheered the athletes onward. My child has found contentment in simply being included.

Life Lessons

How often do we get so caught up in the eventual result of whatever we are engaged in that we forget about the beauty in the process? Regardless of it is career, education, athletics or our everyday search for all mighty dollar, so many times we focus on what we can eventually win or achieve that we forget to think about all of the people, things, and experiences along the way. As we move forward in life may we always be strong enough to follow the lead of a little girl from Van Buren Missouri who has withstood the pain of training, agony of defeat, soreness, and exhaustion merely to be a part of the bigger picture. Hopefully we can stay focused and truly care about finishing the race while embracing all the awesomeness that is present along the way.

Chapter 48

Giving Thanks

As the sun rose on a bright new day, our routine was not unlike any other morning. As we made our way to the Livingroom, my wife noticed something that seemed to be seriously out of place. With the girls tightly tucked into their beds, sleeping, the living room was absent any movement. As we rounded the corner, one item caught our eye. There, lying on the back of the lounge chair was a shiny, rather large, chef's knife. Not the small or medium size knife, this one was the big boy of cooking knives. Curious as to how the knife made its way from the kitchen area to the living room, we were unable to figure it out so we just waited till the girls could shine some light on the question at ha nd.

Later that morning we asked the girls if they knew anything about the knife and Lilli gladly began explaining why it was out of place. She explained, she was minding her own business, in her room when she heard something upstairs. Not knowing exactly what she heard she decided that the safety and welfare of the family fell upon her, so she felt it was necessary to arm herself as she went about the process of searching for the noise she heard. When asked why she had the knife, she explained that she needed to protect everyone. As you could imagine, the thought of a ten-year-old arming herself with a knife, half her size, was somewhat comical yet concerning.

As we discussed the proper responses to strange events and the acceptable tools which should be used, mainly dad, I couldn't help but think about what the child had told me and imagined this little girl, scared, yet digging deep to summons her inner warrior princess to protect her sleeping family, slowly sneaking around, step by step, peering around each corner in anticipation to what she may see. As my heart turned from worry to joy, my mind shifted away from pure awe to that of a realization of how great of a turn my life has made recently.

The past few years, having the girls in our lives have without a doubt added excitement and joy to lives which considered life, already, pretty grand. With each passing day, we find that new adventures are at hand and rarely does a day go by that the antics and actions of these two little angels provide not only inspiration, happiness, and wisdom but likewise, continuity and stability to our exceedingly busy lives. Hearing the giggles and laughter, the playing, and even conniving, creates a mode by which we to find ourselves letting loose and enjoying this life a little more.

Life Lessons

My hope for you my friends is as we approach the holiday season, the new year finds you seeking out the medium by which you can find enjoyment, calm and a bit of inspiration. Welcome change and never neglect the possibilities as they arise. For it is within those same possibilities that we can truly fill the canvas of life with meaningful interaction and events destined to enhance our joy.

Chapter 49

Good Deeds Help Build up Treasures

As I pulled into the driveway, I caught a glimpse of my youngest child hurriedly moving back and forth on the outside deck. When I asked her what she was doing, she simply described that she was gathering acorns. As I reached the door, I was met by my other daughter who rapidly exited the house and at a full gallop, ran to her sister's position. Although I never really considered gathering acorns to be a thing of excitement, the girls seemed to on this day.

Following settling in for the evening I found it odd that I hadn't heard the girls in a bit, so I went outside to check up on them. Finding them scurrying around, as when I last saw them, I asked them if they were still gathering acorns and left it at that when my youngest said she was. Upon returning to the comfort of my couch, I had finally found the perfect positioning, where I would hopefully remain in comfort for at least a little while. As quickly as I had found my perfect spot, the door swung open and my youngest ran up to me. "Come on Daddy, I have to show you something", she bellowed, with a smile on her face, emitting excitement with every breath. As she reached out her little hand to grasp mine, I decided that her desire overtook my comfort, and I willingly came along, voicing my interest in what she had found. She described that she had done a good deed and wanted me to see it. As we walked outside, she led me to a large oak tree where at its base, she and her sister had compiled a rather large pile of acorns.

Upon seeing the stack of acorns my mind simply asked why while my mouth described to the girls that I though their pile of acorns was awesome. Riyann then began describing to me that all the squirrels had been working hard to prepare for winter. She explained that she decided to do a good deed and help put all the acorns in one location to make the job of gathering a winters store of acorns easier for her little friends. You see, she said, "I'm helping them build up treasure".

As I watched the excitement in my daughters' eyes, while they did their good deed, my heart felt a much greater comfort than the couch had provided me a few moments prior. I praised the children and considered the fact that many times, our good deeds may go unnoticed, and the squirrels may never find their treasure two little girls prepared for them. Regardless, the importance lies in the act itself, not so much on gaining recognition for your actions. For it is when we act out of kindness, striving to better the situation for others, building up their treasures, that our own are multiplied. May we all learn a lesson from this simple act of kindness and performing of a good deed. It is when we build up treasures for others that we truly experience the treasure of service unfolding.

The girls check the pile daily to see if their little furry friends partake in the offering laid before them. Thus far the pile hasn't lessoned but I have no doubt that in the near future the squirrels will recognize the gift provided and enjoy a little comfort provided by two little ladies with really big hearts.

Life Lesson

The importance of the lesson lies in the act itself, not so much on gaining recognition for your actions. For it is when we act out of kindness, striving only to better the situation for others, building up their treasures, that our own are multiplied.

Chapter 50

Young Love

The words which every dad of daughter's cringe over became a reality for me the other day. As I picked my children up from summer school, I could see the excitement on the face of my nine-year old. As she stepped up into the truck it was like she was going to burst. Saying our hellos was rapidly overshadowed by her immediate asking "guess what". Sensing that she had a good day, I was interested in what the child had to share with me about her day. Before the words could escape her little mouth, her elder sister, in her best older sister fashion of ruining her siblings surprise, quickly asserted "you're not gonna be happy", as her face displayed a cynical grin. With my interest fully peaked at this point I turned to the child and encouraged her to share her story.

With my excitement growing due to the buildup of anticipation I listened with a smile as the child began sharing with me this thing which caused her to be so overly excited and resulted in this day being the best day ever. Then it happened, the words flowed forth, causing an immediate heat flash to consume my entire mind, boy, and I'm pretty sure soul. As the child, giddily, sharded "I have a boyfriend" I sat speechless, expecting a much more exciting narrative, forgetting what it was like to have the "first love". Understanding that third-grade love is for the most part harmless, I did my best to encourage the child and display some symbolic expression of excitement for her all while dreading the fact that my little girl was growing up. As her sister sat, still grinning, seeming to be waiting for good ol dad to "freak out" and give her little sister a talking to about how Stephens girls find their boyfriends disappear after dad finds out, a narrative I have often passed on to my girls jokingly. Her pleasant anticipation was short lived, and the grin transitioned into an expression of shock when dad simply shared that he thought her finding a boyfriend was great and he was happy for her. Taking a second take, the elder sister could only muster the words... "wait.... what" to dads reply.

Her elder sister's response and confusion stemmed from the fact that when I replied to the newly found knowledge that my little princess had found her knight in shining armor, it was drastically different than when she herself first told her mom and I about a love interest. I routinely joked and discouraged the topic of liking boys; don't you know they have cooties? I know, I know, but come on, I'm a dad. As stated, this time was a little different. For months, Riyann has discussed the fact that she is simply "bummed out" and doesn't know how much she can take because her "little heart is broken into a million pieces" She describes that she has approached a couple classmates, explaining to them that she likes them only to receive the response that they didn't like her then abruptly running away. She longed for the one boy she could call her own just as her friends had.

Seeing the joy and excitement coupled with the fact of truly how dangerous can third grade love be, I simply rolled with it rather than my initial response of "oh heck no". Now my fatherly responsibilities continue so I had to ensure that she knew that although I was happy for her, there were still the rules of engagement.... no holding hands, no hugging.... and definitely no kissing. Shyly, while maintaining the smile of experiencing "the best day ever", she replied that she understood but couldn't promise there wouldn't be at least one "big hug".

As we traveled home, I continued reveling in the excitement my little girl was feeling while laughing a little inside at her sister's continued confusion coupled with excitement because of the newfound love interest. I thought about how truly important it is to allow our loved ones to experience life. Protecting our children and loved ones is a crucial role of every parent. Similarly, allowing them to experience all the special things life has to offer while watching at a distance is encouraging true growth. Growth not only on the part of our children but likewise on our part. Although it seems contrary to my role as a daddy, I find myself hoping for at least one more day before the little boy takes off running and messes it all up, leaving my little princess experiences heart break again. I will have plenty of time in the future to revert to my old nature of chasing them away, for now, I will enjoy the moment.

Regardless, the importance lies in the act itself, not so much on gaining recognition for your actions. For it is when we act out of kindness, striving to better the situation for others, building up their treasures, that our own are multiplied

Life Lesson

Revel in life, hold on to love and welcome kindness my friends. For these are the moments which wisdom is gained.

Chapter 51

Moments of Humor and Confusion

With the dawning of each new holiday season, it always seems that our family experiences moments of fun, frustration, elation, and times when all you can do is crack a smile and hold on for the proverbial ride. This year was no different. Although making a conscious effort to scale back a bit to ensure the girls fully understand that although receiving gifts is cool, the act of giving is the primary focus, considering the ultimate gift we have received. One aspect which always warms my heart is the inclusion of distant family members throughout the season.

Like other years, recently, my wife and I had the opportunity to watch our two grand-daughters as their parents traveled to town in search of the perfect Christmas gifts. As I have aged, I have come to the conclusion that having my two girls, willing to assist us with the task of babysitting the babies is crucial. Where I fully admit, my energy level has been lacking recently, Lilli and Riyann pick right up and ensure that the little girl's excitement and energy is directed in the right direction, leaving the elders to sit back while we watch the chaos unfold before our eyes.

As the one known as dad to some and Popa to others, my main purpose in many instances is to sneak around, feeding the kids candy and then watch as the meltdown of the other adults commence because of the explosion of energy derived from Popa's little surgery gifts. Ensuring that my duties were fulfilled I strategically dispensed cotton candy and leaned back in my chair to observe. Attempting to divert attention, I quickly decided that I may have possibly overdone the candy dispensing so drastic means had to be implemented to ensure I lived to see another day.

It was then that I loudly asked my eldest granddaughter how she was doing and what she hoped to get from Santa Clause this year. Hearing no response, I turned slightly and re-voiced my question. It was then that my mother, who was present, described that the girls' parents choose not to celebrate the holiday with the Santa figure, but rather that he's not real. As my youngest heard this she sprang into action to safeguard her younger nieces.

The words which flowed from the mouth of my child caused me to literally fall out of my chair. Upon hearing the words from her grandmother, Riyann quickly began walking towards her, shielding the younger child, saying "what are you thinking Nene"? feeling that the scolding wasn't enough, she added "you can't, tell a little child that". Stunned, both grandma and I could muster little more than shocked smile as we looked at each other. After a short time of explaining, Riyann came to understood, slightly, what Nene was saying and as she walked away simply repeated "it's just not right".

As the sugar rush subsided that day, parents returned, and the grandchildren headed back home excited for the opportunity to hang out a bit with family. No further mentions of Santa were heard, out of respect, but Riyann continued displaying her dismay over Nene's words, with the occasional head shake and expressions of disgust. As the day drew to an close, I was reminded of the preciousness of life and how, at times, we must boldly come to the defense of our fellow family members.

Life Lesson

Understanding that regardless of the outcomes, we must shield one another from the damaging words and events which strive to steal our joy. I for one find solace in the season and the opportunities to gather. Be on the lookout my friends, have a bit of fun, but remain on guard to protect those we love.

Chapter 52

Its ok

Over the years, my ten-year-old Lilli and I have learned that we enjoy sharing exciting or purposeful videos with each other. I often hear my child, from the other room giggling uncontrollably and know that she will soon come and show me the newest gem she had found. It has become a competition of sorts with both of us attempting to find the funniest media to make the other stand in amazement and add to our joy. The other day, amazement resounded, not through a funny video but because of my having an opportunity to truly gain a glimpse of the heart of the child.

As many of you have learned over the past year, Lilli is a recluse of sorts, centered on learning and excelling through education. Her competitive nature can at times be overwhelming with her consistently attempting to be the pleaser, many times leaving her confused as to why others simply don't see the benefit to treating others with kindness. She has adapted over the years, and learned that she can at times go overboard, treating some with a lack of kindness rendering her feeling down, internally beating herself up.

As we traveled to school the other day, I explained that I wanted the girls to hear a song I had recently placed on my play list. Although not a newly released song, I had heard the song again while searching videos. The song, surely heard by many, was originally sang on one of the recent competitive television variety shows. It was written and sang by a young lady who was battling cancer. Taking the world by storm, the song seemed full of meaning and was generally a good, wholesome song about keeping your mind in the right place.

As I began relaying my interest in the girls hearing the song, Lilli simply leaned back and prepared herself for the pending nightmare she would surely experience. Not being a real fan of dad's music, she routinely listened, to be nice, but rarely enjoyed my taste in what surely was the best musical choices.

As the words of the song "it's ok", by the artist Nightbird began playing, I simply sat back and waited to see what the girls had to say. To my surprise, both Lilli and Riy began singing the song, word for word. After talking about the song, I was amazed that the girls had found the song on the internet and had come to not only enjoy listening to it but also to take the words to heart and strive to live by them. Lilli described that the song was really good. As A father, hearing the words and watching as your children, at such young ages, were able to live their lives with such a mantra was refreshing.

Life Lesson

Understanding that life is inevitably going to throw things at us which routinely cause us to stumble or throw up our hands in frustration is an essential part of healing. Knowing and preparing for the events in life which set us back will undoubtedly allow us to work through those things better. Sometimes, as Lilli, and I have learned, our plans in life are sidelined because of a multitude of reasons. Life simply isn't fair, and it isn't until we recognize the benefit of simply saying It's Ok, or I'm going to be ok, that the process of moving forward truly begins. I asked my child what the song spoke of, and she simply replied that it is about "being ok, regardless", oh what a wise child.

Chapter 53

"It's ok Daddy"

S ometimes it's hard to determine when the roles and responsibilities of parent and child are supposed to begin and end. The manner by which they intersect, and how the roles are swopped, at times is mind boggling. As many of you know, the past couple of weeks have been a series of peaks and valleys for my little family. With the failing health of one of my wife's beloved pets and the loss of two other pets, it seems we are nearing another moment of grieving and loss. Trying to make the best of it, we have strived to spend as much time as possible preparing not only ourselves but the girls for what will surely come. Last night, I sat speechless as my daughter assumed the role of comforter and parent.

Understanding fully that the child has an earnest heart for benevolence and compassion it would have been common for her to do her best to ease the pain of any family member in times of hardship, forgoing her own. What was not expected were the words she chose to utilize to accomplish her goal. As I sat, reveling from the events which had taken place merely moments before, I felt a tiny hand on my shoulder. As I turned, I saw my child, lowering herself to my level so she could impart a small amount of wisdom on her old dad. To fully understand one must be privy to what had happened moments before.

As our eldest pet struggled to maintain life, she experienced an incident where I was sure we had lost her. Working through the wails of loved ones, I worked diligently to bring the tiny pet back to us. After regaining her balance, she rested quietly in her bed while our family quietly ensured she knew she was valued and loved, not knowing how much time we had left with her. Sitting back, doing my best to forgo the emotion of the moment, allowing my girls to have the spotlight to grieve however they chose fit, I sat in silence.

As the little hand rested on my shoulder my daughter looked gingerly into my eyes and explained "it's ok to cry daddy." Doing my best to maintain my stern dad, protector vibe, I smiled and simply responded that I knew, and I appreciated her. She then patted my shoulder, gently, and added "daddy, you are not a cop any more...you can let your emotions out and cry... it's ok now." This little girl went on to say, "It's ok to feel and let your emotions show daddy." As I assured the child that I was alright and how much I appreciated her, I could not help but feel the sting of her words.

For what seems like a lifetime I have filled the role of protector, placing all emotion aside for the betterment of the situation. I have held the lost and dying and put on a welcoming face to ease the suffering of those around me. Not unlike me, many of us worry little about our own personal health and emotion when confronted with the pain of others. We simply fall into the role of protector, strength, caregiver, or father and place our feelings aside in hopes that our strength will have a positive impact on others. But like me, only to be outed by a nine-year-old doing their best to fill our shoes.

My hope is that our children do not have to counsel us on the benefits of allowing our emotions to show at times. For if we remain strong while allowing our pains to release through healthy emotion, it is then that the continuity of the entire family unit can blossom. Will I ever be able to show raw emotion, I do not know, but doubt it. But one thing I am confident in is that I have a little person who has my back and will remind me that its ok. May you find your battle buddy my friends, that one person who through thick or thin can remind you about the value of each other, gently placing their tiny hand on your shoulder assuring you it's going to be alright.

Life Lesson

When moments of frustration, pain, and disaster pile over us we must remind ourselves that it will be ok, and the sun will rise again tomorrow. Finding a battle buddy who will walk alongside you as you traverse this course can mean the difference between success and failure.

Chapter 54

Looking is not Always Seeing

Childhood and the act of parenting are many times filled with countless moments of thrill seeking and adventure. Although reserved by nature, I have been known over the years to join with my children as they engage their adventurous side, holding on with all I had, in an attempt to bolster their exploration while simultaneously maintaining a grip on my own sanity ensuring that no outward signs of fear or apprehension were evident. For as we all know, a dad must constantly be on guard, to ensure their provider, protector image remained intact throughout every moment.

I remember when my eldest child, Natalie, was in her teens and she and I would attempt to go on Saturday adventures, One Saturday we chose to make the short journey to an area widely known as Rocky Falls. The area was a beautiful, National Parks maintained, venue where adventurers could enjoy exploring the beautiful swimming pond, climbing the rocky water fall area which covered a seeming endless expanse, or simply enjoy the view of the creation which lay before you. As we ventured forward the dad in me flowed forth as I felt it was necessary to prepare my child for every possible hazard we may face upon our arrival.

As we drove to the area, my mind couldn't retreat from the fact that recently, our small city had three young children which had been bitten by venomous snakes. This weighed heavily on my mind, knowing that we would be exploring an outdoor recreation area where it wasn't uncommon to cross paths with reptiles. As we approached the falls parking area Natalie continued voicing her understanding at my repeated warnings about the dangers of the outdoors.

Departing our vehicle, the excitement grew as we began the short journey to the recreation area. In the lead, as any good father would be, I continued to bombard poor Natalie with warnings and guidance about the difficulty seeing snakes and the need to be cognizant of our surroundings. I remember looking down to the pathway describing to her how this area is difficult because the common snakes in our area blend well so paying attention was a must. As I continued driving the subject home, the words which came out of Natalie's mouth, as we approached the half-way point on the trail, would become the foundation for a multitude of emotions including fear, embarrassment, and concern.

The words Natalie expressed were simply that as we walked, and I spoke about paying attention and looking intently for snakes, I had stepped on a venomous copperhead snake. Natalie and I froze in our positions and as I turned towards her, standing mere feet away, I observed the small snake flopping around in an evident showing of pain, confusion, and anger. The snake remained alive and directly in the path between my child and me. As I stood in a state of shock over what had transpired, I had a difficult time coming up with a safe resolution. That darn snake remained in our path, growing ever angrier at the fact that a big ol boy just stepped on his head. Escape to the side was futile as both sides were heavily wooded and surely filled with the little guy's buddies. It was then that I devised the greatest dad plan known to man. After carefully inspecting the side of the path I located a fallen limb, small enough to effectively utilize yet large enough to provide a cushion of protection from the reptiles waiting fangs.

It was then that I gently, ok in all reality not so gently but more in the fashion of drunk, crazed prehistoric warrior mode, picked up the snake with the limb, launching him outward to the great wooded unknown where he could recover from his surely likewise embarrassing experience. Once the path between my daughter and I was clear we went about our adventure. To say it was enjoyable would be a lie. I remember the rest of the short journey consisted of a fake smile, hypervigilant watching and truly anxiety filled series of moments where enjoying the trip had fallen along the wayside about the same time as the shadow of the great white sneaker descended upon that little snake minding his own business along the trail at Rocky Falls.

Life Lesson

Thinking about the adventure Natalie and I had that day reminded me that throughout life, many times we are committed to look intently at events, people, and situations in hopes that the truth in any given situation revels itself. There are times that looking simply doesn't reveal the true nature and situation which lies before us. Looking simply is the act of directing our eyes in a particular direction while seeing is becoming aware. Our adventure found me looking intently for any dangers but failing to truly be aware of potential dangers. May our days be filled with awareness as well as direction. For therein lies the benefits of a true adventure.

Chapter 55

Never Accepting Defeat

As my wife and I described ways to overcome difficult times to our child, I could see she was struggling. Not only had there been a total shift in the ways she was used to doing her schoolwork, but the content had also become increasingly more difficult for her. Within her eyes I could see a combination of both frustration and normal pre-teenage defiance. It was evident that she had conditioned herself for defeat because the journey would simply be too hard in her mind.

While weighing the pros and cons of her present situation, my daughter truly wanted to please us, by excelling, but the cost was becoming more and more difficult with each passing day. The things which used to come easy for her were as only a fleeting memory and all that remained was a constant battle between giving up and finding the strength to overcome her challenges, challenges which were growing larger, seemingly with each passing moment.

As I thought about how to help my child conquer the present challenge, she faced, it was apparent that she was suffering from primarily a self-imposed mental blockade which was causing her to have an inability to find even a sliver of motivation. Her frustration and lack of motivation was in turn causing her to spin her wheels in an endless bog of mud, per sa, rather than having an ability to overcome and excel.

I thought about how often you and I go through the same frustrations as we face the bogs in our paths on a day-to-day basis. Unfortunately, maturity and age doesn't cause us to be exempt from struggles along the way. Although we would love to be able to describe how at a certain age or point in our existence, we no longer experience struggles or frustrations but truly, that's not the case. Rather, life it seems, is a constant interaction between good times and struggles, high points and valleys which seem to have never ending walls of crumbling soil where our footing remains unsure, and the security of a solid foundation is just out of our reach.

The one thing we older folks have learned over the years is our assurance that if we merely hold on, if we simply continue placing one foot in front of the other, if we remain focused, we then can and will overcome the valleys in life and ascend the mountains before us. Sure, the times of trial and frustration are not desirable, and many times prove themselves debilitating. But through endurance and perseverance we can and will overcome any challenge we face.

Finding the will to go on as we face the challenges before us is crucial for each of us. For without that will, man never would have stepped on the surface of the moon, said no to tyranny, and had a tea party, stormed the hill at Bunker, crossed the beaches of Normandy, or spoke the words which birthed a movement, "I have a dream". Sharing those tricks and strategies with our younger generations, mentoring them on overcoming their own obstacles does little more than pave the path, deep within each of them to succeed when all seems lost. That my friends is what it's all about. Although my beloved child struggles still, she now has a better understanding of how with each sunrise, a bright new day arrives, full of possibility and opportunity. A day worth fighting for, a day of overcoming struggles and basking in the light of what's to come.

Life Lesson

Find your stronghold my friends and hold on with all you got.

Chapter 56

Never-Ending Inspiration

As I walked through the grocery store awhile back, I saw a friendly face approaching me. As we met, the woman began talking about the latest article in this series which had been published in the newspaper. As she described the joy the articles bring her, she revealed that knowing me and the girls, helps her visualize our stories and causes her to "chuckle a bunch" as she reads about their latest antics and adventures. As we prepared to part ways, the kind lady looked at me and made a statement which cause me to think about the words she spoke. She revealed "you have a never-ending supply of inspiration with those beautiful little ladies" and "you are blessed because of it".

Contemplating her statement, I was instantly brought back to a day several years prior when our family's lives were changed forever. Out of tragedy, lives were changed, sacrifices made, relationships built, and new family units developed. Since that moment, the new beginnings have brought us a seemingly never-ending series of blessings coupled with adventures which not only keep us on our toes but likewise, tug at our heartstrings leaving us with an inability to remember what it was even like before the girls.

Regardless of if it's the silly antics of an eight-year-old, coming into her own, outfits which make you cringe, or a piece of art, created in love, our lives have been forever touched. The years have brought us arguments, smiles, and tears all while providing our family with a front row seat to living room dance recitals to the frozen theme song and other cartoon verses, I'd rather forget, as our beloved children show us the newest thing, they have found joy in. We have played, cheered on, and watched as the family tradition of making good hearted fun of the ones we love is emboldened through a strategically planned practical joke. We do all these things with one intent in mind, that is the intent to enjoy one another and build each up.

My heart overflows as I think about the moments where I have watch true kindness and love flow from the soul of these little, fragile humans, intent on simply bringing a little joy to a world seemingly hardened and course. Considering the words of this friend, my mind immediately flows to the words my wife once said when she told a friend "I can't hardly remember the time before the girls, our lives before them, and I truly don't want to". As far as having a never-ending supply of inspiration, yes, we absolutely do. Our blessings flow repeatedly because of our children. Whether you want to call it luck or design, we luckily are the bearers of these blessings. For it is through these two little ladies that we can get a glimpse into not only what kindness, love, and respect can be but also what inspiring others to a greater level of awareness and compassion entails.

I am a lucky and truly blessed man. Friends, take a moment, close your eyes, and consider the benefit those around you pose. Because at times, when we sit silent, it is then that our eyes are opened to learning and true recognition. Appreciate your inspiration and always take the time to thank them accordingly. They truly do help us rise to a higher level and I wouldn't want it any other way.

Life Lesson

We must take the time necessary to consider the benefit of those around you. When we do, it is then that our eyes are opened to learning and true recognition. Appreciate your inspiration and take the time to thank them.

Chapter 57

Practicing What We Preach

While seated in the truck, trying to find the energy to begin the journey home I listened as my child, out of the blue, began lecturing me on the ins and outs of parenting. With a semi-smile on my face, I couldn't help but be amused as I listened to the child describe her rules as a mother. Without prompting, she began.

When she becomes a mother, she is going to make sure she is not playing with her cell phone while she drives. Ensuring that I understood what she was saying she described it was important to pay attention and concentrate on the road. What made the entire narrative interesting is that for once, my cell phone was holstered, securely by my side. Sensing that I proudly had complied, before being asked to, Riyann quickly shared "you know daddy, sometimes you play with your phone when driving". What's a man to say? After explaining that she was right, and I shouldn't look at my phone while driving because it is a distraction my little angel simply explained that the easiest way was simply to "shut it off". Not taking no for an answer she patiently waited until I followed her direction to make sure we had a safe trip home.

The child then heard the annoying sound of the seat belt warning devise emanating from the dash. Sarcastically, she said "oh this car has one to"? Rule number two, according to Riyann was that everyone, including the driver, must wear their seatbelts. Feeling I could outsmart the child, I quickly preempted any new narratives on my daughter's part by adding my two cents. I explained that she was right, the safest way to travel was by buckling up. Hoping she didn't notice I carried on and placed the vehicle in reverse and began the journey home. Wide eyed and possessing a grin reminiscent to a I told you so grin, the child commenced staring me down. As she caught my attention her eyes moved towards my unattached seatbelt in an evident way of communicating to get it buckled old m an.

Sensing that the learning lessons brought by a nine-year-old had concluded, I breathed a sigh of relief and began attempting to redirect my child's attention to some things which weren't so deep. Capitalizing on her audience, she then stated, "want to know what rule three is?" what's a guy to say? Yep, I excitedly inquired as to what it was. She then explained that our speed was important, and we should never go above sixty miles per hour.

Wrapping her rules of parenting up, Riyann turned to me and asked; "Did you notice I stood in front of you when we were walking to the car?" Explaining that I had, she quickly shared that the reason she did was because if mommy's car came towards us, on accident, she would be struck first. She described that kids need their daddy's so by her saving me, she ensured Lilli would have her daddy around. I explained that her safety was important and that through working together we can all succeed safely.

I laughed as the child began her lecture about her rules of parenting which later took on a somber tone. So often we forget about the fact that our children are listening intently to us even when we feel they are not. Our words and action routinely become their own, if we simply listen. Therefore, we must constantly be on guard, ensuring that our words and actions are suitable for the next generation. Riyann's rules are no different than the rules our family has lived by for the most part. What I've found is it's easy to set rules and begin sharing safety tips with our kids. It is more difficult to follow them ourselves, until a nine-year-old points out the obvious.

For me my children are everything. The thought of losing one is devastating. What we must remember is that to our children, we are their world and as I found, if necessary, they would choose us above themselves.

Life Lesson

Slow down my friends, place yourself and your ease on the back burner as we strive to follow the same rules we have set for our kids. For their safety is our reason for rules, likewise, our safety is crucial to them.

Chapter 58

Reality Reveled

Recently I described my hesitation about truly embracing my daughter's newly found love for cheerleading and their positions of fliers on their team. The big day of their demonstration came and went, unremarkably. Other than a moderate amount of anxiety and "stage fright" because of the large crowd watching the event, the girls performed admirably and came away unscathed. My illusions of bruises and broken bones did not become reality as both girls pretty much followed the direction of their coaches and enjoyed their demonstration. Better yet, good ol', overprotective dad wasn't forced to flash the dreaded "dad stink eye" look at some unsuspecting eight-year-old for dropping one of my girls.

As I sat in the filled gymnasium seats I felt a measure of pride, assuredly felt by the many other parents, grandparents, and friends attending the event in hopes of bolstering their own individual joy over watching their loved one's perform. As the children performed multiple cheer routines, I felt an overwhelming sense of accomplishment for both my girls as they did what cheer athletes do. The excitement of the moment was only overshadowed by my elation over having the opportunity to continue tagging along as these two exceptional little ladies experienced new things while they discovered what would be the norm in their future.

As we traveled homeward, the girls and I shared our thoughts as each girl described what aspect of the evening, they enjoyed the most and for the most part could have lived without. As I listened, my mind quickly jumped to the fact that throughout our lives, we can often fall into a state of permanent self-preservation. A form of preservation where we worry over every little thing, hesitating to fully live our lives and enjoy the beauty it has to offer. As a parent, preserving our children's safety can at times become the center of our universe causing us to think the worst and hinder their ability to prosper.

Understanding that there is no greater duty, as a father than to protect my children, I must safeguard both myself and my children from simply "thinking the worst" and hence not allowing them to experience life because of my fear of the unknown. What I learned from this entire cheerleading experience with my girls is simply that the reality of our experiences is rarely what we envisioned in our minds. Spreading our wings and trying new things, broadens our ability to explore everything this life has to offer and maybe, just maybe our exploration will empower us to greater heights of

awareness and adventure.

Life Lesson

Fear not my friends, the reality of life is our ability to accept risk and embrace the rewards.

Chapter 59

Returning the Favor

As I peered over the side yard, into the dog run, I realized that I had made a huge mistake. What seemed like only yesterday, the memories of erecting a new deck which would enclose my large dogs, brought joy to my heart. Now, looking upon the deteriorated base, holes, and piled up leaves brought only frustration. Not only had the babies who once frequented the enclosure long ago crossed the rainbow bridge, but its intended use had become merely a memory from times past. As our family found a new use for the area, it was my time to shine as I prepared it for our newest family members, a flock of chickens, which would surlily bring both joy and frustration to our family.

What I hadn't realized or truly gave much thought to was the fact that when we neglect something, whether it be an item, structure, or even person in our life, the item quickly loses its brilliance and can easily fade away. Outside debris and conditions wear away at its foundation, and before long, all that remains is rubble. My once brilliant dog deck, a spacious area designed for comfort, had wasted away, all because I had neglected to remove the leaves which had fallen, year after year. So rather than a quick day of cleaning, my task of preparing became a total reconstruction.

As Riyann and I looked over the deck, preparing to begin work, I shook my head in disbelief. My regret over failing to simply clean up, over the years, was evident. As I looked towards my daughter, what I saw was quite the opposite. Affixed to my child's face wasn't regret or frustration but that of excitement and interest. Where I saw work and looked upon it with distain, she saw opportunity. With each screw removed, board discarded, and ugly word muttered under my breath, my child grew more and more intent upon the task at hand. In my frustration, she discovered adventure.

My attention was drawn to the mind of my child as we worked. As with any child, her attention would rapidly be diverted from the task at hand to something much more fun. With each jump and stomp she discovered that she could break the decking, exposing a large hole where a board once lay. The dad in me barked warnings while the daddy in me joyfully watched as the child would move to another location and play the role of a wrecking ball. As we continued our task, I noticed that the fun of breaking trough the wood had run its course and my child quickly disappeared. No, not under the deck, just onto other fun.

It was then that I saw my little girl run to the new wood pile. As I watched her struggle with a new piece of lumber, much larger than her, I inquired as to what she was doing. She relayed that she was bringing me a new deck piece to install, just "doing my part, to help" she said. Deterring her was difficult but she soon returned to my side, finding a new job and purpose in helping.

I learned a valuable lesson this day. So many times, our busy lives, full schedules, and general tiredness causes us to either neglect or strive to quickly resolve the issues in our lives. The last thing we want is to be bogged down with outside influences which lengthen the processes. Although my beautiful child lengthened the process of repairing the deck because of her antics of simply being a child, she made the experience worthwhile. So many times, it has become evident to me that if we merely give those around us our all, they will do as Riy did, and do their best to return the favor. Riy worked hard, tried new things, and had a little fun along the way. She may not have been able to carry a piece of wood twice her size, but she sure gave it a good shot.

Life Lesson

Friends, work at welcoming involvement rather than avoiding it. You too may just find that creating holes, in the end, lay the foundation for bridges.

Chapter 60

Teaching Discernment

When I woke up on Saturday, my day was pretty well planned out. The agenda included a full day working in one of our buildings, trying to finish up the maintenance that I had been avoiding every opportunity I could. As I lay in bed, greeting the new day with all the vigor of a turtle midway through a lengthy journey, I sat up hoping my beloved wife would somehow save me from the fate she had been reminding me about for weeks. To my surprise, she did in fact extend the life- line I was seeking. Her recommendation that rather than working we head out to town and do some shopping, rested on welcoming ears and without any prodding I was ready and willing.

As our little family drove from store to store, the girl's excitement grew. Each new experience, regardless of how routine, seemed to enhance the girl's vigor for learning and socialization. As we traveled through one specific parking lot, I observed a scene from the past. As a young child I routinely remember seeing cars with their trunks open. Inside the trunk was always a cardboard box with the words "free puppies" written on the side. Seeing the words, as a child, lit a flame of excitement for me and I routinely ran to the area after begging mom to let me look at the precious little furry bundles.

Seeing a vehicle parked, trunk open, and that recognizable cardboard box caused me to smile and quickly say "look girls, free puppies". My words were met with silence initially, then, as soon as they saw what I was talking about, pleas of taking home a new family member. After momma and I firmly shot down that thought, the girl's excitement continued as we talked about free puppies. As we spoke, I noticed Lilli, my middle daughter, shift into a solum mood and grow silent. With concern in her eyes, she peered at the vehicle and puppies as if she feared something unknown.

It was then that it hit me. Routinely, in an attempt to protect our children, we joke about avoiding vans with free puppy's signs. We have told the girls that it is important to never go anywhere, or get to close to strangers, because you never know when they may be up to no good. Our experience that morning of seeing, in real life, what we had been warning the girls about seemingly hit home to Lilli. As we inquired as to what was wrong, she somberly admitted "mom, I would have gone to see the puppies". She went on to describe how the desire to see the puppies and maybe even hold one caused her to totally forget about all our previous warnings, inevitably succumbing to the puppy wielding bad guy hoping only to snatch her up.

The events which unfolded that morning reminded me about the importance of protecting our children while laying out realistic views of what they face in an age-appropriate manner. For Lilli, every person who may be giving away free puppies were dangerous and out to swoop her up. In reality, while the danger exists, understanding that all strangers aren't bad is imperative. The key to her understanding was to instill the fact that resting upon mom and dad's wisdom would enhance her own discernment.

Learning when it's safe to engage a stranger is at times difficult. Instilling in the minds of our beloved children when its safe and potentially dangerous is hard. As I've said in the past learning from those around us is an imperative part of growing up and truly benefiting from our community. Teaching our children indicators of potential dangers although difficult is essential at fine tuning their ability to discern when and where they should avoid.

Life Lesson

As we strive to prepare our kids for life it's important for us to set the tone for safety while avoiding putting out a blanket of totally sheltering them from everything that is out there. Some people giving away free puppies are good people simply trying to share their merchandise. Walking alongside our children as they learn the fine art of discernment not only ensures their protection, but also gives us the opportunity to love on some babies, receive puppy kisses, and feel the joy of our childhood regardless of how far removed we are. Walk along for the journey my friends.

Chapter 61

Teaching Them to Survive

Several years ago, I was relaxing at home, minding my own business. My eldest daughter, Natalie, was out doing something and I was simply soaking in the fact that I had no pressing items on the agenda. As I sat, peering out the window, I watched as a vehicle pulled into the driveway, parking directly behind my vehicle. As my curiosity grew, I observed, a child, known to me as one of Natalie's friends, exit the driver's side of the vehicle and remain near the front. I noticed the young lady had a look of confusions mixed with a moderate amount of fear gleaming from her face. Being alone at home, the situation required the easing of my curiosity thus I decided to go outside and see what was troubling the child.

As I exited the front door the young lady turned and looked towards me. Describing to her that Natalie was not home she simply looked at me, acknowledging my comment yet still appearing confused. As the two of us remained in the driveway, hem hawing around, I was no closer to understanding why the child was in my driveway and what she needed. At this point it was apparent that I would need to transition into a different level of communication, plain talk, so I simply blurted out "what do you need sis".

The young lady quickly turned to me; the look of confusion on her face turning into a look of embarrassment, as she appeared to be carefully choosing the next words which came forth from her mouth. I helped her along and said, its ok, do you need help? At that, the child described that she was almost out of fuel. Relieved that the child wasn't about to disclose something more damaging such as our pending destruction, or imminent danger I simply responded ok. Like clockwork we transitioned back into to the silent oddity of no words. Uncomfortable with the fact that I had not been able to ascertain exactly why this child stood in my driveway I asked her if she had the money to get some fuel and she replied that she did. Explaining that her father had provided her with his debit card for fuel, paying for the resource was not a problem.

As we continued the process of my attempting to resolve this issue, which was taking away from my relaxing, carefree day, The child turned to me and with what appeared to be a broken spirit, explaining that although she had all the necessary provisions for fueling her car, she did not know how to do so. Taken back, I stood there for a moment and thought about my next move. Without hesitation, the child and I embarked upon a fifteen-minute lesson on using a debit card at a gas pump, opening the fuel door, and fueling her vehicle safely. As the child listened intently, I became vested in her success and hoped our lesson took hold and the child was wiser than when she awoke.

I could see that a load of fear had been lifted from the child's shoulders as she pulled out of the driveway. As she left, I felt a sense of pride in the fact that I was able to be the means by which a neighbor could excel. My mind rapidly flowed to that of my own concern as to whether I had adequately prepared my child, a junior in high school, just like her friend.

As parents we often go about our days determined to ensure that our children are prepared for their future. We lecture about principles, teach higher learning, centering upon history, reading and math, all the while forgetting, many times, to prepare them for the basic life skills they will require.

Life Lesson

How often we overlook the little things, the basics, the tire changes, jumping batteries and fueling a vehicle. In a life where toasting bread, balancing our bank account, understanding bank interest, or even cooking a turkey has taken a back seat to standardized testing and the computerization of society we must lay the foundation of survival for our children. For without a firm understanding of the basics our children are destined for potential failure in this thing we call life. Friends, take time this week to teach a life skill to our little ones. Trust me, teaching your child how to check her oil will save you in the end.

Chapter 62

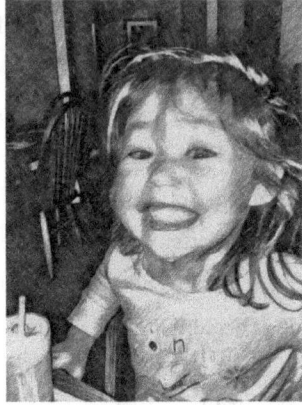

The Gift of Gab

Recently, our travels brought us to the Branson Missouri area, enjoying a little down time with our family and close friends from the past. As with many previous journeys, one day was set aside to hit the nearest retail outlets in hope of finding that most desired but least needed item we just couldn't live without. Recognizing that the venture would be less than ideal was apparent as the traffic into the outlet mall was horrendous. Regardless we ventured onward. As we searched for a place to park our vehicle the girls grew ever more excited at the sight of all the storefront decorations. Equipped with the knowledge that mom and dad were for the most part push overs, they knew they would be reaping the rewards of a shopping spree. The girls silently did their best to hold in their excitement and wait for the treasured spot to begin their adventure.

Following a moderate amount of searching, our parking spot was secured, and the doors opened allowing the girls to escape their momentary confinement and unleash their pent-up shopping demons. Our first stop was a clothing store. Upon walking through the entry doors, my heart sank as I saw the mass of human bodies hustling around, apparently thinking it was black Friday. This vision, coupled with making the mistake of looking toward the check-out line, which I can honestly say, snaked around many displays reaching from the front of the store to the rear of the shopping area, caused my mind and body to instantaneously experience an overwhelming feeling, only describable as the feeling a prehistoric warrior, being hunted by a wooly mammoth, would have had.

As we carried out our exploration, we got to the point of checking out when I, putting on my best husband face, decided to take one for the team, told my wife she could co sit outside in the fresh air while I checked out. To my dismay, she gladly obliged leaving my youngest daughter and I to traverse the dreaded, seemingly endless line in a somewhat symbolic test of wills, manhood, and perseverance. As my wife departed the store, smil e affixed, I did my best to wrangle the eight-year-old, wild-eyed princess who was simply taking in her surroundings.

It was then that I heard my child say "hello, I really like your scarf... its very pretty". As I turned to see who she was speaking to, I observed a middle-aged woman who kindly responded to the child in an appreciative manner. The comment my child made to the stranger was not uncommon and did not come as a surprise. As many of you have learned Riyann is a loving soul who simply desires to make people feel special. What stemmed from the original compliment is what left me speechless and gleaming with pride for my child.

The next forty minutes entailed Riyann carrying on a conversation with this woman, and the woman responding back to her as if they had been acquaintances for a lifetime. The two spoke of clothing design, school, where we lived, why we were there and every-thing else under the moon as the child directed the conversation. Mid way through the conversation I listened as this eight-year-old looked up with enchantment in her eyes and simply said "would you like to be my friend?" As I glanced at the woman, as I had many times to ensure she was not bothered by my child, the woman smiled and responded that she would love to be her new friend. The two continued their conversation as the kind woman spoke of the importance of being kind, family, and hair styles. As we approached the check-out Riyann turned to me and asked if we could let her friend in front of us since she had less items. As quickly as it began the newly blossomed friendship came to an apparent end as the two said their goodbyes along with wishing each other well. I thanked the lady for talking with my child as she assured me that their conversation was just what she needed, and she would treasure it as I should treasure this wonderful human child.

As I exited the building, I experienced a momentary sense of shock coupled with contentment leaving me honestly unable to find the right words to describe. I had just witnessed the most beautifully perfect interaction between two strangers which ended in a friendship that both would surely remember, and I would never forget. Upon re-gaining my senses, I thought about how important it truly is to simply be kind, take the time to engage others, and to be approachable. No-one, including me would have blamed the woman if she wouldn't have engaged my child in conversation, she could have easily responded to the initial compliment and then turned away avoiding further communication, but she didn't. Rather, she allowed my child to engage her and she, with kindness allowed a blessing for herself and a child leaving with a feeling of importance and worth. Just think about how effective we could be in our communities if we merely slow down, lower our phones, make contact, and enjoy simple conversation with others. As the woman described to me "a little kindness goes along way… and it makes the line mov e faster".

Life Lesson

Be kind my friends, take the time to engage, you may just find a blessing in the form of a stranger.

Chapter 63

There is Joy in Silence

Sitting in the car, I looked at my wife. Her eyes caught mine and it was evident what was running through both of our minds. As we traveled homeward following a long weekend of working at the motel, our children, securely buckled in the back seat, carried out their normal routine. Our youngest worked the events of the past day through her mind, quietly. Her sister on the other hand, similarly, worked through her daily adventures but chose to express them vocally.

What has become a norm for our family, our ability to share with one another our ups and downs, our joy and strife, has also brought with it a bit of humor at times. Our ability to find enjoyment from the little things this life has to offer has added to the bonds we have fostered with one another. Although emboldening most of the times, humor sometimes overtakes the routine, leaving us with a sense of overwhelming contentment and awe at how our children respond to their everyday lives.

One constant throughout this entire form of interaction we have as a family is my daughter's uncanny ability to speak for long periods of time, uninhibited, and for the most part lacking any true substance other than her desire to be heard. This gift of gab per sae, has left her mother and I amazed at the child's ability to go on... and on... and on. Finding humor in this gift, my wife and I have attempted to focus the child and even tagged her with the nick name of chatterbox in an attempt to teach her that everything in moderation is more preferrable than simply speaking without ceasing. As you can imagine, our attempts have failed as the child's persistence has prevailed. Fine tuning her ability, she has taken her gift of gab to an entirely different level, which I must admit is truly impressive for the most part.

As we drove home, this gift of gab was on full display. Initially talking about her new swimsuit, she quickly transitioned into a one-sided discussion about the weather, her friends, and the turtle she saw along the way. This, the turtle story, grabbed the attention of her sister who immediately began quizzing her about the creature, to our dismay. As my wife and I grinned, we decided to see just how long the child could keep going. Making multiple detours we continued driving to see if our lovely daughter would tire. As we concluded, what seemed to be our longest trip home something amazing happened.

Out of nowhere, our child stopped chattering and silence resounded. Shocked that the gab had come to an end, we looked at each other like victorious warriors. We had conquered the endless gab session and found the key to a quite ride home.... Simply keep driving. Our joy at winning the battle and surviving the endless gabbing was short lived. As we sat in joyous silence, out of nowhere our little angel spoke these words "so yeah, my day was pretty fun, guess what else I did". With that, we were blessed to learn more about the interworking's of a ten-year old's life. As a loud, audible sigh from our youngest could be heard, we sat as the story again reveled itself in all its glory. Grateful for the blessings, even the long-drawn-out ones, of being able to hear our child tell her story.

Life Lesson

In life, there are benefits to being able to communicate effectively. As we travel this road, our ability to surround ourselves with a group of people who care enough to listen is crucial to our wellbeing. Fine tuning the skills necessary to share our message while learning that some moments require us to simply sit back in silence, listening, is important. Although humorous and truly overwhelming at times, I wouldn't replace the moments we share with our little chatterbox for anything. Teaching her about the joy of silence is secondary to the happiness we derive from hearing her personal accounts in all their splendor. Welcome the chatter my friends even as we desire the silence. For we never know when the chatter will subside, leaving us with a longing for the day we can hear those words one more time.

Chapter 64

The Pain of Defeat.

The weather was perfect, teams assembled, and strategy designed for our girls as they stood at the starting line on their second to last cross country meet of the year, last week. Lilli, feeling the confidence from an astounding second season's performance was sure that she would not only medal but could possibly pull out a win if she played her cards right. The days leading up to the event, she repeatedly described to her mother and I that she was happy that her hard work had paid off and she would medal in each race this year. Disregarding our warnings about becoming overconfident, Lilli maintained her view, shrugging off our warnings as misguided or simply the views of old people who really didn't know.

As the race began, the girls maintained their positioning as was normally seen in the previous races. Midway, it was apparent Lilli was struggling as the race took a unique turn with the athletes failing to thin out near the front. Shouting words of encouragement, we encouraged her to "pick it up" as the final stretch was drastically approaching. As the runners began racing across the finish line it was apparent that our little runner would not medal on this day.

Awaiting our youngest child's finish, I struggled to catch a glimpse of Lilli to no avail. As Riyann crossed the line, touting a personal best finish, I could then move to the area the students were assembled. Providing support and congratulations to Riyann, my heart was softened by the smile on her face. Her pride was beaming as the spectators congratulated her and shared the same smile which was unavoidable upon seeing her. It was then that I felt the tight grasp of Lilli as she grabbed on tightly to my waist, burying her head in my side.

Feeling her disappointment, I attempted to console her through explaining that winning a medal is not the gauge for success. I explained that if she knew she gave it her all then she was successful. Looking up, she described that she simply didn't understand. "I didn't medal daddy; I had my strategy down and I just couldn't do it ". As we spoke the agony of defeat was evident for this little girl who had become accustomed to a great deal of success. It seemed no amount of encouragement was going to lessen the sting for her and seated in silence, eyes closed, while the medals were awarded, Lilli became a true legend in her daddy's eyes. Lifting her head high, the child congratulated the girls who had beat her and carried on, pinpointing what went wrong and planning her strategy for the next race.

As I watched my child experience the pain of defeat, I remembered my own experiences during my childhood where it was a relative certainty that I would win and did not. The pain is not unlike real life events where we experience loss and are left with the undesirable task to carry on. In that moment, the moment where we only feel like retreating within ourselves, avoiding the reality before us, our response is imperative. For Lilli, her grief was short lived as she immediately decided she disliked the feelings she was experiencing and became determined to overcome in the next race. The key, as her mother guided, was not to overcompensate.

Life Lesson

Life carries with it loss, pain, and events which bring forth disaster in our eyes. The key is to recognize our loss, pick ourselves up, and be reserved to the fact that we will make it through the pain to win again on another day. Stay focused my friends, life can beat us from time to time. The important thing is the means by which we respond to the beating and our enduring the negative while embracing all the good which lies ahead. Keep moving forward!

Chapter 65

Things Better Left to Others

As a father, it is important to not only be present and active in our children's lives but also to do all that we can to help their mother along the journey. I remember, as a young man, working alongside an older gentleman at a large apartment complex in Colorado. My excitement was evident as I prepared to welcome my first child into this world. Seeing my readiness, the old man decided to provide me with some words of wisdom as I prepared to embark upon the journey which would forever alter my life. Seated in the break area, the old friend looked at me and said three words which remain with me to this day. Rick, he said, actively take part. He described that his first child came with excitement and old-world beliefs, so he really didn't help his wife much. He said the late-night feedings, dirty diapers, and general play was left totally up to his wife. As the child grew, he explained, he had a good relationship with her, but he soon noticed that anytime the child needed anything she turned only to her mother.

If she scraped a knee, she ran to momma. When she needed help, momma was the answer. The old man shared with me that although his wife was more than capable of supplying for all the child's needs, he felt like a hole of emptiness filled him each time the child was in need and would avoid him and run to mom. He went on to describe that when he received the news that his wife was expecting a second child, he decided that he would take a more active role. He shared with me that upon finding out about his soon to born second child, he began committed to be involved not only with the second child but the first as well. He told me about when his second child came along, he took an active role. He took part in the early morning changings, feedings, and day to day interaction with the child. Getting on the floor became an everyday occurrence as he played with the child on her level. My friend described that his simple commitment resulted in not only his beloved wife receiving much needed help, but with a stronger bond between a father and his children.

As I welcomed my children into this world, I consistently tried to follow the advice from my old friend. Not only did I realize he was totally right, my interaction with my children not only broadened the bond with my children but likewise relieved some pressure from my spouse. This parental action carried over to my girls. Although I wanted my wife to experience all the pure awesomeness of parenting her first diaper bound, non-walking human, whose only desire, evidently was to hamper her sleep and cause her to forever remain in a state of cleaning up, I knew good old daddy had to lend a helping hand. My interest in being the proverbial co-helper, intent upon living out the dream of being the perfect loving, caring, and attentive husband and father reached its tipping point one afternoon as it routinely does at one point in our children's lives.

As parents routinely do, my wife and I had devised a game of sort surrounding the dreaded changing of the diapers. Alternating the "changer" duties, I found myself next up. As we relaxed, post dinner, I noticed something quite particular tickling my nostrils. Doing my best to ignore the odor, it became unescapable. The simple tickling evolved to an outright assault as if I was being stuck by the heavy weight champion of the world. Hoping that my loving wife would likewise notice the unavoidable stench, and find pity on my attempts of avoidance, I stood by trying to act like I was busy with something. With a grin on her face, my wife saw right through my feeble attempts, and simply said "you're up". Reserved to my pending fate, I embarked upon the inevitable and rounded up my beautiful little daughter who evidently had exercised her internal demons on that day. What I soon encountered was a situation that all my years preparing to be the best father ever neglected to cover. To lower it to the simplest terms, I couldn't hang. As I lay the child down, cleaning wipes in hand, I began the process of changing the child. Although routine, this time it was different. As with the professional hunter, what is seen is not always the reality. Seemingly a routine diaper change brought with it a toxic bioweapon camouflaged superbly, which caused me to jump back, unable to fulfill my mission. Although giving it my best shot, I ultimately had to call in back up, retreating to a place of cover, and fresh air, as momma quickly swooped in, rendering the area safe.

We joke about situations throughout the journey of parenthood. Some good, some bad, but ultimately these are the times of building bonds and living the experiences. Not unlike parenting, there are times in our lives where some things we face are undesirable, but we must give it a shot even if we eventually come to the conclusion that some things are best left for others to experience. Being a father, playing with my kids, and molding their lives is an honor I would never change. Taking part in the little things have allowed me to broaden my experience level and feel complete. With that being said, I'm forever grateful for those heroes who have swooped in and saved the day when I simply couldn't.

Life Lesson

Working together with others who bolster our capabilities, or simply pick up the slack when we cannot, is the truest form of commitment, trust, and teamwork. Be ever vigilant my friends.

Chapter 66

Unexpected Gifts

As I traveled home the other day, I began thinking about how truly blessed and how totally undeserving I really am. As many of you know, my little families' lives were changed drastically in 2015. Prior to that day in March, life was good. I had successfully completed my stint as a single father, raising my daughter to become a successful citizen. Maintaining contact with my daughter Natalie, became routine. I never allowed a day to go by without contact. This was rather burdensome for my adult child but knowing it helped satisfy my longing for her safety she appeased me by always answering my call. I had done my duty and now had the fortunate task of moving forward with my new life, hoping to one day welcome grandchildren, and simply said, centering on myself.

Life was good. I met the love of my life and began settling into my new life. New goals and aspirations began unfolding as we planned for an early retirement. Hoping to get away from the center of town my wife and I decided to begin researching properties in rural Carter County. Out of nowhere, a beautiful home, a great deal larger than we needed became available at a low price so we jumped on it, purchasing the home.

Looking back, our life truly fell under the watchful eyes and design of God. For what we didn't know was that this four-bedroom house we just upgraded to from a two-bedroom home would soon be put to use in a way neither of us could have imagined.

Our being content in our circumstances rapidly changed with a phone call from the Highway Patrol. What we couldn't expect that Sunday morning was that the trooper within minutes of taking the call would be in my home, describing how my brother, his wife, and three of their eight children had been killed in a motor vehicle collision in Lawrence County Missouri. Reeling with shock, I simply did what I have become known for, I put it all aside and began caring for my family as any good cop would. I remember the nigh our lives changed vividly well. Lying in bed, with one of my brothers two orphaned girls in a crib near our feet, my wife turned to me and described that we knew what we needed to do.

This same woman who had never bore children, never felt the joy of motherhood, never opened her soul in that manner, had lowered her proverbial barriers and opened her heart to two little girls. Within months, we would become the parents of a smiling one year old and an inquisitive two-year-old. Through tragedy the lives of multiple people were changed. The home we purchased was now filled not only with two little angels but with laughter, joy, and the sounds of family love. The woman I was fortunate enough to find has welcomed motherhood exceptionally and the girls have enhanced the lives of so many through their joy, compassion, and kindness.

I often think about the blessings I have received in this life, and simply sit in reverent appreciation. Looking back now, I can visualize how everything aligned perfectly for my little family. Events and circumstances, years prior, set the foundation for our life today. My wife and I joke often about how when she chose me, she never could have imagined the turn her life would take. In reverent excitement she simply replies, when I joke, that she wouldn't change a thing because in us, she found true life, true peace.

Life Lesson

So many times, we question why things happen the way they do. Many times, we are left with a lack of understanding. What I've learned, simply, is the life I knew before the girls was good. The life I have now far exceeds any expectation I ever could have imagined. The greatness of life as a father has been bestowed upon me once more and I will revel in the opportunity with each passing day. Welcome the unknown my friends. For it is in the opportunities that we can find true peace and true blessings.

Chapter 67

Working Through Fear

Have you ever had a moment when it was simply difficult to put into words what you were feeling? Today is one of those days for me. As I relax, thinking about which new adventure, silly antic, or everyday happening I wanted to share with my friends today, my mind is flooded with ideas, yet consistently wrapping back around to my appreciation. I remain amazed about how two little lives can bring so much fulfillment and joy to a person's life. Regardless of whether it's the words, spoken by a nine-year-old, which stop you in your tracks, holding back the laughter, because in your child's words you hear yourself, or through the actions of the older child, scolding the youngest for a misstep in the same manner you, yourself were scolded many... many years prior, the gift it seems is in the journey.

I am reminded of a modern-day meme which is circulating throughout the social media genres... although simplistic, the meme is powerful as it describes "The most powerful jewels you'll ever have around your neck are the arms of your child". Countless times, this past week, I have been stopped in my tracks over the words and actions of the girls. Not stopped because of angst or frustration but rather pure, unabridged joy. Yesterday was a prime example of this unavoidable, overpowering excitement and love for my children which cause me to consistently feel blessed.

As I arrived home from work yesterday, I was met by Lilli who immediately reminded me that I had promised she and her sister that they could drive the golf cart around the property when I got home. Felling less than motivated to do so, I began thinking about the most believable excuse which would put off the inevitable for one more day. As I conspired within myself in an attempt to find a way out, no suitable thoughts which would allow my rapid exit rose to the surface. Reluctantly, I agreed and we were off. As I exited our residence, I had to chuckle a little as I saw the girls seated on the cart in the ready position. Riyann was perched on the back seat, taking her place, waiting patiently for the festivities to begin and her to turn to shine. Lilli on the other hand was sprawled across the driver's seat, trying her best to appear relaxed and void of excitement as she waited for good ol dad to start it up. Ushering Lilli to the driver's seat we were off. Remarkably, the first several minutes of the girls driving were and quite relaxing.

It was then when little Riyann took the wheel and with excitement beaming from her face, began the process of driving. As we rounded the corner, I was amazed at how well each girl was doing. Out of nowhere, Riyann pushed the brake bringing the cart to a stop and with an apprehensive smile on her face described that she was done driving for the day. Confused, I turned to the child and asked her if she was sure, and she replied that she felt she had driven enough today. As I looked at her, I could see she gazed ahead and seemed to be fixed upon a vehicle which was parked on the lower portion of the parking lot. It was evident that the child's fear of the newly changed course caused her to forego her desire to be behind the steering wheel and simply resign herself to not taking the risk. Recognizing this face caused me to encourage the child to continue onward. With a little encouragement Riyann started driving again, ever so cautiously as she conquered her fear of the new rock in her path, overcoming adversity, and simply feeling the enjoyment of new experiences.

A sense of pride came over me as I tagged along with the girls as they sharpened their golf cart driving skills. What made the afternoon even better was the fact that unlike the other times, I felt no fear. Allowing myself to give in and take part, leading the girls as they improve their skills not only enhanced their experience but also allowed me to tag along while their confidence grew.

Life Lesson

In life we face obstacles. Some large and some small. The key, in my mind is our ability to face those obstacles, overcoming them as they pass by, while we travel the rocky road of life with those we love. Center on the little things my friends. For when we recognize that we and we alone are major influences relating to our children's success it is then that it all comes into perspective.

Chapter 68

Taking Time to Reflect

D riving down the highway, headed to our next appointment in a city a couple hours away from home, an interesting sight revealed itself. The words "would you look at that" emanated from the back seat, catching my wife and I's attention. As we turned our heads to look, Lilli said that she couldn't believe how many birds she was seeing just hanging out and flying around. As the flock caught my eye, I noticed a great number of winter geese, some bedded down in a field, and some in flight overhead.

As we sped by, the geese left our sight as soon as they had entered. Although menial to some, the opportunity to see the fowl provided our family with the opportunity to find a little enjoyment out of a rather monotonous journey. As we completed our business and headed back home, later that afternoon, the geese again entered our view. As the family began looking in awe at the creatures the excitement-fueled conversation began between the girls and their mother. Feeling that we had been faced with not one but two opportunities to expand the girl's knowledge, I quickly decided to pull our vehicle over to the emergency shoulder so the girls could not only see the birds better but likewise hear them.

As we sat, the girls discussed the beauty of the flock as their mother described the sounds, they heard were the birds communicating with each other. I watched as the girls each lifted their cameras and began taking pictures of the wondrous sight. Chattering about the differences, commonality, and pure enormity of the flock was only overshadowed by the intermittent giggles about the manner by which one bird would interact with the others.

After about twenty minutes, discussion waning, and pictures taken, we pulled back into the lane of traffic and headed homeward. Although miles away from the muddied flock of geese, their memories remined vivid in the girls' minds as they continued talking about what they saw. As we arrived home, my wife turned to me and relayed that she felt we had a good day, and the trip was enjoyable. I couldn't help but think about what a great opportunity we had to strengthen the bonds of our family while taking a few minutes to stop and learn.

The small act of pulling over to the side of the road so the girls could truly experience the huge flock caused us to be behind schedule but in the full scope of things had no bearing.

Life Lesson

So many times, we get so caught up in the day-to-day happenings that we fail to take the time necessary to experience life alongside our loved ones. Slow it down a bit my friends. When the opportunities to broaden our children's experiences and knowledge reveal itself, jump right in and guide them through new adventures into a life of true learning. They are worth it.

Chapter 69

Learning the Old Ways

T his year had been full of new adventures and learning for our family. One of the things we were determined to accomplish, as we undertook this home school journey with the girls was that we hoped to not only enhance their book knowledge but also subject them to real world learning. We found ourselves pointing out new and exciting things to the girls while we simultaneously drew reference to how the new adventure could be applied to life. Our approaching the girls learning in this manner has opened the doors to the kind of great conversations and enjoyable responses and application that only a nine- and ten-year-old can provide.

Early this week, one of those learning opportunities presented itself. Upon speaking to another home school family, it was decided that it would be beneficial to gather several home school families together and have a lesson on the old way of making butter from scratch. I must admit that when my wife first approached me and told me about the field trip I got a bit of a chuckle out of it. My mind instantly flowed to my childhood when my own mother decided that we were going to churn some butter to avoid the rapidly growing prices at the store. I remember being filled with excitement over the process, at least the first few minutes of the adventure. After that, arms sore, from repetitious shacking and mind weary from utter boredom, I lost interest and hoped only for finishing in record time.

For me the end product was simply not worth the time it took to create. As I thought about the girls taking part, my mind immediately took me to my experience, and I immediately grinned over the thought of what the girls would soon experience. In the end I was sure the lesson would prove beneficial to them, but the process would surely be a battle of wills with the girls loosing focus rather rapidly, and everyone looking on made aware of their displeasure.

As I eagerly awaited word on how the lesson went, and how the girls performed I found myself again thinking about my own experience as a child. Looking back I am glad my parents took time to include me even though I'm certain they could have accomplished their task with ease and in half the time absent my complaints. My inclusion provided a window into a small portion of the past. The experience, although silly to me, allowed me to learn an important skill while also gaining an appreciation for the tings those who came before me had to do to survive.

As the girls returned home, I inquired as to their experience. My youngest, as expected, described the process was long and boring and the bread and butter were terrible. My middle child, gleaming with excitement, described it was the best experience ever and she loved the fact that we could do so much with one simple product. Momma had a blast watching and leading and felt the butter the group made was spot on and some of the best she had tried. As I listened to the girls tell their tale I was glad that this simple little project dreamt up by a couple loving mothers would now spark a desire to learn more about the old ways of doing things.

For it is in the past that we can learn a lot about our futures. It is in taking the time to show our children the good and bad, the easy and difficulty of generations far removed that our children could become more well-rounded and appreciative. Our girls now understand what it may have been like for some people generations ago and in doing so have found a new appreciation for where we are today.

Life Lesson

Share with our future generations about the past my friends. It is through learning that understanding begins.

Chapter 70

Friends Come and Friends Go

I woke up a couple weeks ago to a text message from my sister describing that a large branch had broken off one of our trees. The branch, while falling, happened to strike our new vinyl fence, destroying one section of the fence. Although not happy with what had happened and the money it would cost for repairs, I decided to take it in stride. I promptly picked up my phone, got on my social media site and like seemingly everyone else does now days, posted about the incident. Instead of being negative I shrugged the start to my morning off and decided to turn a negative into a positive and joked about how it was going to be an awesome day and how thankful I was for the blessings I receive daily.

The next couple weeks were filled with clean up, ordering supplies, and awaiting the faithful FedEx driver who would be bringing my new fence panels. Upon their arrival and as everything else fell into place I set the date that I would try my hand at repairing a fence. Becoming somewhat of a handyman, my wife has become accustomed to my fixing things around the house rather than paying someone to do it. Whether this newly acquired skill set is a blessing or something entirely different is yet to be determined.

Hearing that I was going to be working on the property, my youngest daughter decided she was going to accompany me to assist. Her tagging along has become a norm and to be honest a bright spot for me as I approach the challenges of building maintenance. Additionally, her presence helps remind good ol dad of the importance of watching my tongue while struggling to complete projects given the stressors only a handyman dad can understand.

As we began the process of preparing materials, I noticed my child doing her best to help lift a box of fence panels. As I thanked her, my attention was drawn away from ensuring I didn't trip over the uneven footing, to her location behind me. As she quietly said "dad, check this out". As I looked, she directed me to a tiny, baby lizard which had taken up residence on top of the box I was carrying. As we watched the terrified creature, I did what dads do best and recommended that she find a container to house her new friend. With zero hesitation the child bolted out of sight, quickly to return holding a mason jar. The next several hours consisted of dad working on the fence and Riyann helping while taking routine breaks to check the welfare of her new friend, Bonzo the lizard.

The child worked hard at making her new friend comfortable, ensuring that it had food and water and everything a lizard needed to survive like a king or queen. Research using Seri was a norm as I heard the child ask her iPad everything from what Bonzo liked to eat, drink, and the best time for him to nest in his new home. Seeing the joy in the eyes of my child while playing with her new friend was refreshing. Later, my lovely child and I would discuss survival and fairness to wild creatures. The discussion led to my daughter somberly walking into a wooded area and releasing her new friend. A short time later I watched as my child sat in the driver's side of my vehicle. As I opened the door, I could see tears in her eyes as she thought about her lost friend.

As I thought about my child and her pain over doing the right thing by releasing her new friend, the realization came to me that friends come and go from our lives routinely and we so often are left hurting by their departure. Although we know that they are in a better place and that conditions are many times much more aligned for their success, our struggle is not lessened. The hurt we feel is real.

Life Lesson

We must remind ourselves that our loss is in fact not final. For the memories of our friends and the times we have shared remain. It is through those same memories that we can find the courage to care again, love again, and reach out again, building new friendships along the way.

Chapter 71

Unplugged

For over a year, a running joke in our family has been that this weekend we are going to be unplugged. Although a novel concept, turning off all electronics and centering on getting back to the norm of yesteryear where social media, text messaging and surfing the World Wide Web were all nonexistent and merely a grander thought of futuristic dreams, it is a bit more difficult than one would think.

I have routinely thought, and even joked with others, about how purely insane our lives have become, tethered to the seemingly restraining power of electronics. It seems like not long ago I was filled with excitement over my newest toy; a bright shiny bag phone issued to me by the Gilpin County Sheriff's Office. While engaging in the act of simply plugging in the power source and screwing in the affixed antenna; I would be instantly tuned into a world not unlike the one I viewed on the television and be unrestrained. Today, it's difficult to imagine a day, or moment without one.

Not being restrained and reachable has become a concept far removed from our current cultural norms. In many instances, we have a generation walking amongst us who are willing but unable to visualize the very concept because truly, that old life was never a part of their existence. The thought of leaving all electronic equipment at home and not engaging is wrought with fear, cold sweats, body tremors, and ultimately disabling anxiety. Which brings me to the rest of the story as once coined.

This past week, the girls and I decided that we were getting away for a week as a reward for another school year accomplished and in preparation for the summer rush at the Motel. My wife had the novel idea that she wanted to truly "unplug" and spend the time in a fashion unlike any other family vacation we had experienced. This time would not only allow our little family to become engaged with each other more readily but also allow the girls to experience a time where the real things in life were important rather than then spending money and shopping. Nestling down with a good book, playing board games, and doing some fishing were on the agenda and I can truly say; I was all in, yet we had to ensure that adequate Wi-Fi access was achieved at our destination, you know, in the event there was an emergency.

Our arrival came without a hitch and as we traversed the rocky gravel driveway leading to the cabin, merely feet from the lake, a sense of relief flowed over me. The cabin was modern, yet secluded, quiet, yet clean. A secondary sense of relief came over me when I viewed the beautiful, grey sphere affixed to the roof top, which would undoubtedly allow me to view any emergency weather information coming in our direction, compliments of satellite television.

Unpacking and getting settled in was a joyful occasion as the girls explored their very own "big girl" bedrooms and the expansive living quarters. Surveilling the lay of the land per se, revealed that many before us must have had the same idea of unplugging considering the mere number of puzzles and board games prominently displayed throughout the cabin. Then the thought overtook me… why would there be such a large quantity of "Unplugged" games and offerings in our modern times. As the anxiety began to surface and the feelings of unease began overtaking me; calmness resounded upon the sight of a small black box with flashing lights. My relief of seeing the Wi-Fi box was evident; so, I would need to truly hide my joy and disguise my elation as that of calm approval. As I voiced my pleasure at the location, I simply advised my loving wife "Oh yea, there's the Wi-Fi if needed later on".

As we continued getting a lay of the land, I, utilizing my best tactical prowess, obtained the password and sneakily entered those golden Wi-Fi characters into my device, purely for the reason of obtaining emergency information …. truly, that was why… I'm pretty sure. It was then that I realized the heavenly sight of the Wi-Fi box was merely a ploy to drive a modern man insane because to speak in kind terms… it didn't work. A lack of Wi-Fi combined with the cellular service being barely existent, it was looking like the week would be interesting to say the least.

The sweats returned, carrying with them a series of body tremors, as the thoughts of being able to spend a week without searching social media and maintaining a knowledge of what was going on combined with the inability to check security devices were becoming more and more of a reality. We would definitely have to have a meeting of the minds to discuss the next plan of action to ensure our families survival through this challenging time.

A quick meeting of the big people minds revealed that one device received telephone service and one text messaging, so we were not totally doomed. Then in a cruel kind of game, or possible punishment; we found that media reminders and notifications would occasionally be received; carrying with them a slight teasing of content, unretrievable by our hands given the restrictive "unplugging".

In spite of our electronic isolation our family prospered and laughed more, played more, talked more, and even explored more than ever before. The lack of content and our hands being free from the small chains we seldom recognize caused a growth of sorts within us. Our daughters were able to see that fun can be had by other means than spending a dollar, attending an attraction, or enlisting the approval of a silent few on social media. We ate together, played together, and simply laughed.

Life Lesson

This series of events recently, taught me several grand lessons. New personal firsts can be experienced for you, your children and those you love, if we just take the time to set down the electronics and center on our loved ones. Although it's hard to believe that in so few years; we have become so dependent upon our accessibility we can find true, lasting joy from simply taking the time to put it all down for a moment and center on the person, the surroundings, the experience. I would be lying if I said "unplugging" was easy. For me it was necessary, for a moment. The experience will not soon be forgotten, and I can see more unplugging in our future, as you and your family should.

Chapter 72

Goodbyes are Hard.

As the evening came to a close the feeling of sadness filled the air. What had been a week of joy and utter elation quickly transitioned into a solemn mood of downright depression for the girls. In the morning their storybook week would come to an unfortunate end with the departure of their siblings. Doing their best to put aside their knowledge of their brother and sisters heading back to their own home in Florida, the kids did their best to get the maximum amount of horseplay before bedtime.

The past week had been different from those before. Often, when the girls' siblings visit, the normal infighting that siblings often experience was not present. In its place was seven days of continuity, agreement, and outright fun. The bonds of family had been strengthened and learning new things became common place between the herd of children occupying the Stephens property. Although as parents, we prepared for the normal backlash of behavioral issues that often result following a week with siblings, the pulled heart strings were unavoidable as I looked deep into my children's eyes. Within their eyes, the joy had been overtaken by the expression of sadness from their temporal los s.

As with each time before, the girls will recover and become stronger because of their time with family. The memories of another opportunity to strengthen bonds will reign supreme before long. But still, the moment is a tough one. It seems that no amount of convincing that everything will be alright, no tricks, strategies, or attempts to prove that they will survive fall upon welcome ears. Time it seems is the only thing which will lessen the feelings of loss.

Sitting down, this week, to write a column for a local newspaper, I felt the same sense of loss and sadness. As I rendered memories of my past with my father to paper, my gladness that the suffering ceased and I had the opportunity to learn so much from the man was overshadowed by the knowledge that the hugs, words of wisdom, and smiles would be something I would have to wait for from now on. My temporary loss, with his passing, would forever be my plight yet eternally be his joy at no longer suffering. Loss and goodbyes are difficult.

For some, the loss builds, for others it remains a constant. One person quickly recovers while another just can't pull themselves out of the chasm of sorrow. One thing I know for sure my friends is that although difficult, goodbyes are simply a state of mind. For me, I choose to not look at them as permanent, rather I center on my belief that goodbyes are temporary. If sorrow stems from a loss the knowledge of an eventual reunion lessons the burden.

Life Lesson

Goodbyes are hard, there's no way around it. The key to overcoming the feelings of loss is centering on the journey. Remembering the roads traveled, smiles shared, touches felt, and experiences we have together. It is then that those goodbyes seem a little less imposing.

Chapter 73

Learning New Things

It seems that the longer you live, the more you find out about the dastardly deeds the little angels, in the form of your daughters, did along the way. I spoke a couple of years ago about how my youngest daughter took it upon herself to help her classmates, when she was in kindergarten. We found it both humorous and fascinating that she was dealing out chocolate candy to her friends whose mothers didn't allow it. Over time, the rebel in the child subsided and the corner candy slinger ceased her operations.

The other day I learned about the time the pent-up rebel side of her sister revealed itself. As my wife and I sat at the house I was not so intently paying attention to the conversation my daughter and her mother were having. As the conversation turned to laughter I focused on the girls and asked what was so funny. It was then that momma described to me the lengths Lilli would go to during her preschool education.

Through tears of laughter, I learned that Lilli and her friends had a propensity to ChapStick during that time. Thinking nothing of this newly learned factoid I simply shook my head and listened intently. Lilli continued. She described that she learned that her friends would give pretty much anything for the cherished stick of flavored wax, so she devised a plan to become rich. Capitalizing on her newly discovered commodity, Lilli gathered every tube around the house and went about her newly found job of distributing.

As she described to me that "Kids will trade anything to have some" my mind became confused as to why the children desired ChapStick so much. The thought crossed my mind that maybe the classroom was dry, and the kids needed the moisturizing effect. Beyond that I was at a loss. It was then that I decided to suck it up and ask the child why everyone wanted it so bad. It was then that the pure, unabridged, truth was revealed to me.

Lilli described that the small tube not only provided a soothing level of protection whenever needed, but in addition to that it seconded as a quite tasty little treat, "especially the flavored ones". Speechless, what's a dad to say. As I sat there in non-belief, all I could muster was "really"? Lilli described that the "treat" aspect was truly what drove her success because her product was in high demand, and she had a hard time keeping a adequate supply.

Still speechless, all I could do was shake my head, hold back the laughter, as I attempted to visualize a bunch of three- and four-year-olds slinging Chap Stick in the school yard playground, all to fill their internal need for a waxy snack. Kids today are just plain different. I guess I should be happy that it was my child who had the vision to bring the product to market and then followed through on that vision.

Life Lesson

So often we think about something that is innovative and fail to act. It is when we dream and when we act that we can find success through newly opened doors. Lilli assures me that her slinging days are behind her but admits that there is the occasional temptation for a minty snack. Like I said, Kids are simply made different these days.

Chapter 74

Making Living Worthwhile

The stage was set. Our girls had begun their day the same as they had numerous days before. With all the hustle and bustle of getting ready this Monday seemed the same as every other. But on this day, it would be different. Unbeknownst to the girls, their elder siblings would be making a trip from Florida to spend a week with them. We kept their arrival from the girls in hopes of creating a little surprise from them and to be honest, to see the big smiles which would surely result.

As the girls rode with their mother to grandma's house, the only thing they knew for sure was that they would hang out with grandma until their mom got back from an appointment. The plan was working perfectly. As the car pulled into grandma's, the girls suspected nothing. Entering the residence, the girls, being herded in the right direction, entered the living quarters. Within seconds the girls recognized their brother and sister and joyfully welcomed them while giving their momma a little bit of a hard time, jokingly, for keeping their arrival from them. Momma experienced a bit of joy as well, gloating that she finally was able to be the parent who witnessed the excitement and joy first, before good old dad, I didn't mind, she earned it.

As the day played out it was a beautiful sight to behold. The children interacted perfectly, and the love and excitement were evident, emanating from all involved. Through the hours of swimming in the pool, sharing stories, and walking down to the local shop to get some ice cream, each of the little ones seemed content to simply bask in the perfectness of the moment. As the day ended one of the girls shared with me that they had just experienced "the best day of 2023". She said that she was so happy and couldn't have asked for a better experience "It was the perfect day". The glow of pure joy was soon overshadowed by a cloud of exhaustion as the sun set and the girls drifted off to sleep with smiles on their faces, surely dreaming of the new day to come.

Life Lesson

I thought about how perfect the entire surprise was and how the adventures they had with their siblings had been truly good for the girls. The entire day reminded me about the importance of making time for the people we love, no matter how busy we become. Our ability to surround ourselves with people who have no other purpose than to lift us up and increase our happiness is essential. Because in the end, it's the people who we share our lives with that make living worthwhile. On this day I watched as two teenagers welcomed the play of children, engaging with each opportunity as two much younger children looked up to their elder siblings with pure elation at simply being in their presence. May your day be filled with the love and the presence of those who raise you to a higher plane, my friends.

Chapter 75

Sometimes Trying New Things Expands Old Bonds

As I sat in my living room, relaxing, thinking about what the next morning would bring my beautiful wife described that the girls decided that tomorrow we would go as a family and get pedicures. This adventure was not uncommon for the girls. They routinely make plans for the heavenly procedure once every couple months. My part in the adventure routinely consisted of sitting from a far, watching and reading or simply vegging out. Understanding this fact, I didn't really give the process much thought. At least until the girls elaborated more fully on exactly what would be expected of me this time.

As the girls overheard their mother describing the plans to me the girls rushed to our sides. Without hesitation, the girls explained that I've been working hard this summer and I too could benefit from some pampering so I would be required to take part in the family adventure this time. Like finely tuned warriors, ninjas maybe, the girls sensed my introduction of excuses and countered them with a wide gamut of solid facts and their rationale behind my taking part, refusing to take no as an answer. Seeing that I was making no headway, I reluctantly agreed to lay aside any fears and embarrassment and take part in the adventure.

When we arrived at the spa location, I will admit I was a bit nervous. Not nervous about the act of receiving a pedicure or some stranger gazing upon my fifty plus year old feet, but rather the true possibility that I would be the only male in the room and open myself up to the possibility that one of my friends would see me. For many, a man getting a pedicure is no big deal, for a crusty old, retired cop, being seen by his fellow cops getting beauty work done, well you know how that might go over at the station house.

Mustering every bit of strength, I carried on. How bad could it be? It was early, surely the place would be empty, and my family and I could quickly get done, the girls would be happy, and we would be on our way. As I entered the door my worst fears were brought to the surface. My wife disagrees but I'm pretty sure I heard the gasp from the multitude of ladies as I walked in. To my dismay the place was full of ladies, some getting nails done, some feet, some I have no Idea what was happening, but it didn't look good. All silently looking at the sole man daring to enter their peaceful, man free, domain.

Luckily, as I played it off, I met a few ladies who were overly kind, and supportive, although I'm relatively certain my nervousness became somewhat of a game for them watching along wondering when I may break. With each joke and comment they became more and more emboldened, warning me about the upcoming portion of the pedicure process and how although unpleasant, in the end it would be worth it.

Life Lesson

The act of taking part in an adventure which the rest of the family gets so much enjoyment out of was, in the end, fun for me. By taking part, letting my walls down, I was able to not only strengthen the bonds between my family and I, but also met some genuinely funny souls along the way. So often we hesitate to step outside our norm. Our fears, or overall comfort tend to supersede our willingness to experience new things. When we do, it is then that the doors are opened wide to fully experience life and smiling alongside two precious little souls because we tagged along and were willing to lay aside our comfort for their happiness. I'm not going to say pedicures will be a thing for me in the future. But for this day, our adventure was pretty ok.

Chapter 76

Patience Reveals Truth

As I listened to my ten- and eleven-year-old battle it out, verbally, about silly things like who was wearing whose clothing, why the other choose to look at her sibling in the manner she did, and just how "rude" her sister was being, it took all I had to maintain a levelheaded demeanor. I could barely grasp the constant bickering, demeaning, and outright meanness spewing forth from my babies' lips. The fact that these two exceptional little ladies had stooped to such depths astounded me. With each nitpicking word, adverse gesture, and crossed look my blood began to boil. Unsure at what direction the battle, between the girls, would take, I felt it may be time to intercede to ensure the words being said didn't turn physical. Although I would admit, seeing my pre-teens transitioning from trash talk to all-out battle did pique my interest at who would prevail the victor given no one got injured.

Although I am a firm believer that there are consequences to the words we say, I just couldn't follow through with my belief that if someone pops you because of your demeaning words to them, you learn a valuable lesson. Battling the desire for the girls to learn, coupled with my hope that my girls remain injury free, the time had come for me to put my two cents in. As I reprimanded the girls, I began describing how important family was and how many times it was only our family which has our backs. My words were met with distained looks and constant "well she" statements. As my words remained flat within the minds of the girls, I had no option other than doing what we parents do... I began threatening that if things didn't change, I was going to change things.

As good old dad began listing things he was going to take away, the girls stood with an air of cockiness about them. They had heard the words before and seldom experienced the consequences because dad has a problem with following through when confronted by the winking eyes of his little princesses. Isn't it funny how follow through is not an issue unless it is intended for someone, we hold dear? As I walked away, I continued to feel my heart race and blood boil. I sat and pondered how we were going to get through to the girls when my oldest, from the other room said "dad, it's normal, it's like what you use to do with Aunt Donna". The words stopped me in my tracks and as I turned to the child, holding back my desire to laugh, I simply responded "no, baby, its not the same. I would have been picking myself up off the floor if I said that to my sister".

As the evening continued the girls made up. The angry words were replaced by giggles of excitement over how the sister mastered a new trick on her bike. My frustration transitioned into appreciation as I thought about how fleeting our frustrations can be if we only keep them in perspective. For me, the momentary frustration of hearing the girls fighting, as siblings do, was overshadowed by the true nature of each child. The unkind words gave way to pleas for help as the child saw her sister struggle with a broken bike chain. The negative actions transitioned into helping hands as hair needed braided and make up needed applied.

Life Lesson

Oh, what a lesson we can learn from our children. For it is when we remain patient and understand that with each moment therein lies an opportunity. It is through our patience that we can embolden ourselves to look beyond the negative, forward towards the future, leaving our frustrations in our wake.

Chapter 77

Protecting Arms

With the Cross-Country season drawing nearer the girls decided that it was time to kick-start their training. This season Lilli had heard that the middle school and high school athletes choose to complete their training in the mornings so following suit she has decided she needs to run in the early morning to Riyann and I's dismay. To many, losing an hour's sleep is menial, but to me, at this point in life it has become ever increasingly more difficult to drag myself out of my bed, but I do.

As we began the day's journey, last week, I noticed that the Ozarks were in a special form. The beauty of the early morning ambiance coupled with an opportunity to tag along with the girls was all the payment I needed. As I trailed the girls, of course from the comfort of my air-conditioned vehicle, I sucked in my surroundings and found some quiet time to reflect.

As I watched the girls run, I noticed movement from my right side. As I attempted to focus on what I was seeing I observed Lilli, the older of the two, rapidly extend her arm towards her younger sister. At that moment, what I saw moving became apparent. The girls had come upon a bedded deer. Startled, the deer leaped from its space of comfort and ran off. I watched as Lillie's attention was drawn to the deer and her first inclination was not of herself and her safety but that of her sister.

I will admit I was a bit surprised by Lilli's actions. Being normal adolescent children, the girls go through the routine love hate relationship between themselves. At that moment, all angst, dislike, and frustration between sisters were placed on the back burner and her only purpose was to protect her sister from what unknown creature lurked in the woods.

As I watched Lilli extend her arm of protection, I thought about just how often I do the same. Seemingly a pure reaction, I have extended the same arm of safety with each yellow signal light, close call, and poor driver, to the person sitting in the passenger seat. Although fully understanding that in the event of true trouble the simple gesture will bear little significance other than a valiant attempt, the action seems to have been hard wired deep inside from my father and surely passed on by his.

Life Lesson

Let us consider the true benefit of extending an arm of protection to others. For it is when we reach out in an attempt to shield another from pain that our true sacrifice is viewable. Thinking about Lilli's attempts to protect her sister reminded me of the ultimate reason we celebrate the Memorial Day holiday. For countless men and women, they extended their arm in an attempt to ensure that you and I could rest easily in the comfort of safety and protection. Their gallant efforts cost them everything and paved the way for each of us to live life to the fullest. Lilli could have done very little to shield her sister from danger, but she gave it her best shot. May we always show a willingness to extend an arm of protection to those around us. Even if the threat, discomfort, or scary things run the other way, others can rest easier with the knowledge that we have their backs. Rest easy my friends.

Chapter 78

Walk Your Own Path

I could hear the excitement in my daughter's voice as she ran down the stairs. As she turned the corner and ran up to me, I couldn't help but wonder what had transpired to bring such a smile to her face. Holding a small piece of paper in her hand, I listened along, as she described that she has her very own fairy. Read it she squealed, thrusting the handwritten note towards me. Over the next minute or so the father's heart filled with not only excitement for my youngest child but also pride in the anonymous actions of her older sister.

You see, my youngest is a loving and kind soul who is interestingly both outgoing yet shy, open, yet reclusive in many ways. Finding enjoyment in anime, weaponry, and ancient samurai battles, she has become somewhat of a different kind of child leaving her elder sister to experience a level of confusion she just can't wrap her mind around. Being concerned that the child's fellow students and classmates might find her "weird" her elder sist has repeatedly attempted to subject her little sister to the finer things, more acceptable things kids wear and do. To no prevail, the little girl just continues along the path that brings her joy, caring little about what the world around her thinks.

As I read the words of the note, it became obvious what was happening. The note introduced a visiting fairy, named Sparkle, which had been traveling around and came across little Riyann and decided that she would be the perfect friend. Sparkle shared about her life and the things she liked to do. Centering on the fact that she thought Riyann was special and "very cool" the fairy described that she would forever walk alongside the child even if she couldn't see her. Taking it a step further, the fairy explained that she imagined the family may be going shopping soon, so she left the child sixteen dollars to spend on something very special.

As I did my best to share my child's excitement my mind found it extra special that the exact amount of the monetary gift given to Riyann from Sparkle just happened to be the same amount her sister had received from tips, that day, after helping in the family restaurant. As the child quickly retreated to her room to write Sparkle a thank you letter, I simply thanked Lilli, her sister, for her kind gesture. With a smile on her face, and a little shyness, she described that although she doesn't understand her sister sometimes, she simply needs to feel comfortable being her.

Life Lesson

The lesson good old dad learned from the entire Sparkle incident was quite simply the fact that we all walk our own path. Some paths are difficult, some are easy. Mine is different from yours and yours mine. The things you enjoy may differ but, in the end, they are yours and nobody else's. The fact that we differ doesn't lessen the validity of our life, choices, or desires. When we can embrace our differences and look no further than ensuring that we strive to lift each other up, it is then that our paths become a little bit smoother.

Chapter 79

A Win-Win is Always Best

As the sun peered through my blinds, I welcomed the new day. Still sitting on the foot of my bed, I gingerly tried to dust off the cobwebs from a great night's sleep. As I sat there, I could hear movement from my youngest daughter's bedroom. Within moments I fully understood that this solemn moment of quiet reflection would be overshadowed by the pure action-filled ambiance only two young children can provide. Still, I reveled in the moment.

Shortly, my attention was drawn to my left. As I turned, I saw my youngest child standing with her arms spread wide apart, in an apparent attempt to stretch out. Saying good morning, I was unable to remind her to get ready for church because before I could say the words she inquired as to if I liked the outfit she was wearing. Little did I know that her evening had been filled with planning the next day's outfit to ensure she looked presentable for church Sunday morning. As I turned further, I noticed that she was wearing one of her elder sisters' older, hand me down outfits.

I expressed my pleasure at her choice of clothing and added the fact that the outfit looked like it was comfortable as well as very pretty. With a big smile, she agreed that the outfit was in fact "very comfortable". As she continued speaking about the clothing, I noticed that her smile became enlarged with seemingly each sway from side to side. As she looked up towards me her words caused me to reciprocate her smile. "Thank you, daddy" she said, "it's really a win-win for me, both pretty and comfy, it doesn't get much better than that".

What's a man to do other than agree with those words of wisdom. To the child, although old, the clothing was new to her and bore significance because her older sister gave it to her. This same person she fought with, pranked, cried with, and became angry with had given her a prized outfit and now she too, could be fashionable, just like her sister. As I watched this simple event play out, I was reminded about how our outlook is many times dependent upon our perceptions of worth. To many, the old outfit was simply one of many articles hanging in a closet but to some it is the perfect item. Things many feel are used up or worthless become treasures to others.

Life Lesson

Like Riy's outfit last Sunday, finding worth in things others may feel are worn out can create within us a win-win situation where we can truly benefit from providing new life to someone's hand me downs. Regardless of whether the item is a piece of clothing, tool, toy, person, or wisdom from the past. Worth remains within the eyes of the beholder, creating a win-win deep within our heart, if we simply open our eyes and envision the possibilities of rebirth.

Chapter 80

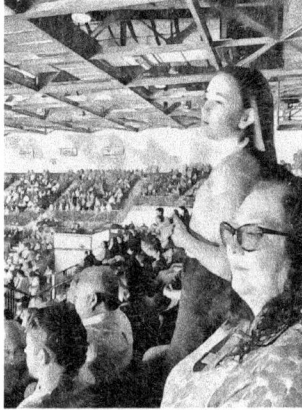

Choose Your Time Wisely

U pon returning home this past week, from working at the motel, the girls quickly ran outside to complete their chores so they could get back on their iPad and watch some more movies. As Riyann ensured her chickens had water, Lilli began the process of walking the garbage bags to the dumpster. The scene had played itself out many times so for dad and mom, it was rather uneventful. At least that's what we thought.

No sooner than I had sat down, I saw the front door swing open briskly. As the door opened Lilli ran into the house, announcing that there was a huge raccoon stuck in the dumpster. The look on her face revealed that she was both concerned and startled by the little bandit who was surely just trying to forage for a bit of human food. Being concerned that Riyann may have heard the commotion and in her special way, disregard all words of caution and attempt to take hold of the cuddly creature, I rose and began quickly walking outside.

As I arrived at the scene of the trespasser, I called for Riyann who to my surprise was oblivious to what was going on. As I cautiously peered over the edge of the dumpster my eyes were met by the eyes of a struggling juvenile racoon who appeared to be struggling from the intense heat and an inability to climb out of the slick metal walls of its once bountiful eating spot. Ensuring that I fully understood its anger, the beautiful creature voiced its disdain for me, spreading its arms as if to tell me to bring it on big boy.

As I summoned the girls, I quickly retrieved a piece of wood and positioned the girls where they could see the animal while remaining at a safe distance. A short time later I placed the wood inside the dumpster and back away. Within seconds the little racoon, using the wood, climbed out of the dumpster, looked at us and call me crazy, but I'm pretty sure it flashed me a head nod before ran off into the woods. As the girls described how cute the racoon was Riyann quickly ran towards the house.

Within moments she reappeared holding a plastic bowl which she had filled with water. When asked what she was doing, she replied that the racoon was thirsty, and she was taking it water. Despite my warnings not to follow the racoon, Riyann began tracking the exact path the creature took as it fled. As she neared the tree line, she placed the water on the ground and gingerly back tracked, ensuring she didn't scare the animal. Proud that she had did her best to help the parched animal, Riyann cared not that she had lost sight of it, only that she had did her best to help it.

Life Lesson

I remember hearing once that "money comes and money goes, but time only moves in one direction. All we have the power and influence over is what you decide to do with the time you are given today". As I think about that truth, I am reminded of Riy's decision that day. For her, the most important choice she could make was to help a struggling creature. Likewise, you and I must find it within ourselves to utilize the time we have to truly make a difference. Our decisions of how we respond to others, how we fill our day, and what we hold dear to us will surely set the tone for our success or failure. Use your time wisely my friends. Look beyond self and into the possibilities of doing good as the time ticks on. For in the end, maybe, just maybe, the mirror will reflect a lifetime of service to our neighbors and a genuine commitment to all.

Chapter 81

Fluff

Scary Things

With the longer days of summer upon us the girls have found joy in simply exploring. Trekking into the woods surrounding the house has added to their adventure and their mother and my anxiety. Seemingly, through the girls' eyes, each new tree provides an opportunity for climbing, each rock pile, a new hill to hike, and each creature the perfect stimuli for their young inquiring minds. The ever-present threat of snakes, ticks, mosquitoes, and chiggers does little to hamper the spirit of our two Ozark g irls.

As the sun began to fall last week the routine was unbroken. The girls headed out as normal and for the most part I expected, like always, to hear the joyful laughs and banging of branches as has become routine throughout their adventures. On this day it was a bit different. Just before dusk the door swung open and Lilli, my middle child, excitedly said "you have to check this out". As she hurriedly walked to my chair, she raised her iPad and began describing this "strange creature" she had come across during her hike.

She began playing a video she had recorded upon encountering this unknown creature. She described that she was walking along and heard some rustling in the leaves. According to her she investigated the noise and "saw the strangest thing she has ever seen". On the screen of her iPad, I recognized that this strange thing she saw was simply an adult armadillo foraging. As Lilli spoke, I couldn't help but smile at the thought of just how strange an armadillo must look to someone who had never seen one before. Lilli continued to describe how the creature could care less that she was there and just walked around "sniffing the ground all crazy like".

Life Lesson

As I explained to her all about the animal she encountered, I thought about how often we encounter things throughout our lives which take us out of our comfort zone. Experiencing something for the first time can be frightening, leaving us hesitant to explore the entirety of this awesome world God had provided. It's only when we restrain our fears and look on in excitement over the experience that we can truly allow the full potential of exploration to be felt. Remember my friends, "life is short, and the world is wide". Allow each adventure to teach us, lead us, and shape our worldview. When we do, it is then that we broaden our understanding and sometimes, every now and then, we can chuckle at the silliness which lies before us.

You make me
shine more then I've
ever shined before. You make
me smile, smile bigger th[an]
I've ever before. You make
me cry cry harder the[n]
I've cried befor. Out of
happiness that I got to
see you once more.